Ecclesiastes for the 21ˢᵗ Century

A Guide to Finding Direction in the Chaos of Today's World

Debb Boom Wateren

Table of Contents

Introduction

Greetings, fellow time-travelers of the 21st century! In a cosmos filled with memes, hashtags, and emojis, where the echoes of ancient wisdom can sometimes seem as distant as your favorite band's first album, we're about to embark on a cosmic escapade to rediscover Ecclesiastes – the OG of philosophical brilliance. Prepare for liftoff because we're about to hop on the wisdom shuttle, and trust me, this one doesn't require a DeLorean.

Now, you might be pondering, "Ecclesiastes? Isn't that the book with all the 'a time to weep and a time to laugh stuff?" You nailed it! But hold onto your AirPods, my compatriots, because this ancient manuscript is ready to unveil some profound insights that even the trendiest influencers might want to include in their Snapchat stories.

In a realm where TikTok trends change faster than the latest iPhone model, Ecclesiastes stands tall as the OG influencer, dropping scrolls of wisdom before influencers knew what "scrolling" even meant. It's like the granddaddy of philosophical Instagram captions, offering more than just aesthetically pleasing life advice – it's got substance, depth, and a surprisingly low count of cat videos.

Why Ecclesiastes, you inquire? Well, think of it as your timeless Sherpa, guiding you through the treacherous peaks and valleys of modern life. Whether you're navigating the life of adulthood, dodging the pitfalls of social media, or contemplating the meaning of life in the short span of a Snapchat streak, Ecclesiastes is your philosophical spirit guide, and it's cooler than your favorite podcast host.

So, my fellow digital pioneers, as we kick off this odyssey, we will use the New Living Translation of the Bible. A Bible made for the 21st Century. Also, remember that Ecclesiastes isn't just a relic from the biblical archives; it's the original life hacker, dishing out wisdom for the ages. Get ready to LOL at the absurdities of existence, ROFL at the pursuit of meaning, and perhaps even shed a tear at the beauty of life's most puzzling mysteries.

This journey isn't about delivering sermons from a pulpit but deciphering ancient scrolls while sipping on our modern-day lattes. So, slap on those noise-canceling headphones, queue up your favorite playlist, and let Ecclesiastes guide you through the ultimate mixtape of life's crescendos and decrescendos. Welcome to Ecclesiastes for the 21st Century – where ancient sagacity meets Gen Z vibes. Let the interstellar adventure commence!

Picture yourself scrolling through the cosmic timeline of Ecclesiastes, not as a lecture from a drab professor but as a cosmic voyage with the universe's coolest tour guide. Ecclesiastes isn't just the wise elder; it's your philosophical wingman, offering sage advice without a hint of condescension.

As we dive into this celestial journey, let's first unpack why Ecclesiastes deserves a front-row seat in your existential playlist. Imagine Ecclesiastes as the cosmic playlist you didn't know you needed, each chapter a carefully curated track that resonates with the beats of your life. And while the book might lack the glamour of an Instagram story, its wisdom packs a punch that would make even the trendiest TikTok dance go silent in awe.

Overview of the Book's Structure

Hop into the DeLorean, time-travel enthusiasts! Our expedition kicks off with Ecclesiastes 1 – a time loop that echoes life's repeating seasons. Picture it as the universe's original algorithm, where sunrise and sunset, memes and counter-memes form an intricate cosmic loop. Your latest viral post? Just a blink in the grand cosmic feed.

Now, fasten your seatbelts as we warp into Ecclesiastes 2 – In a time where success is measured in promotions and LinkedIn connections, Ecclesiastes drops truth bombs that'll make you reconsider your career trajectory. It's a reality check, reminding us that climbing the corporate ladder might be an endless uphill treadmill with no off switch.

Transitioning to Ecclesiastes 3 – Imagine this chapter as the pulsating rhythm of life's events, each verse a dance step in the grand choreography of existence. It's a mixtape where joy and sorrow, likes and dislikes, blend seamlessly into the fabric of our fleeting mortal dance.

Now, groove into Ecclesiastes 4 – Confront the vanity of comparisons in the era of Instagram filters and Facetime. It's a reminder that the real masterpiece is crafted in the authenticity of our connections, not in pixel-perfect snapshots of our digital selves.

Next on our time-travel escapade is Ecclesiastes 5 – Join the journey of responsibility and stewardship. As climate change dominates headlines, Ecclesiastes whispers about vows to protect the cosmic home we share. It's a call to action, where even the smallest eco-friendly choices send ripples through the universe.

Transitioning to Ecclesiastes 6 – Brace yourself for a reality check in a society obsessed with accumulating cosmic bling. Ecclesiastes reflects on the hollowness of chasing material gains without true fulfillment. It's a reminder to find genuine connections in a world blinded by the dazzling allure of social status.

Ecclesiastes 7 – The unpredictability invites us to a cosmic poker game where the cards are dealt with an unpredictable hand. In a world addicted to certainty and control, Ecclesiastes nudges us to embrace the unexpected, finding beauty in the chaos. It's an ode to the exhilarating uncertainty that makes each moment a surprise waiting to unfold.

Now, prepare for the time-travel leap to Ecclesiastes 8 – In an age saturated with information, Ecclesiastes invites us to sift through the noise, seeking wisdom that transcends ephemeral trends. It's the quest for timeless insights in a world where knowledge often evaporates like stardust in the cosmic breeze.

Journeying into Ecclesiastes 9 – In a society thriving on hierarchies and power structures, this chapter unveils the universal truth that time and chance don't play favorites. It's a reminder that the stage is open to all, regardless of the roles we play in the drama.

Ecclesiastes 10 – The wormhole of folly and wisdom navigates us through the minefield of decision-making. In a world where information overload clouds judgment, Ecclesiastes provides a compass for distinguishing blunders from enlightened choices. It's the manual for navigating the digital labyrinth without falling into the black hole of foolishness.

Approaching Ecclesiastes 11 – Imagine it as the stock market of life. Each decision, each investment, shapes our portfolio. It's a call to weigh the risks and rewards, making choices that resonate across the balance sheet of our existence.

Finally, we arrive at Ecclesiastes 12 – It's not just a finale; it's the climax, the zenith, the magnum opus of wisdom. In a world drowning in opinions, Ecclesiastes 12 invites us to distill the cosmic symphony into a melody resonating with our essence. It's the ultimate guide to living a purposeful life, a roadmap to dance through the ballet with grace and intention.

But our time-traveling adventure doesn't conclude here. As we bid adieu to the scrolls of Ecclesiastes, we enter the grand finale – the conclusion. It's not the end; it's a launchpad for further exploration. Consider it not as a final curtain call but the beginning of an ongoing cosmic conversation.

This conclusion isn't wrapping up Ecclesiastes like a neatly packaged gift; it's extending an invitation to dive deeper. It provides a star map for further study, a compass for navigating the vast universe of wisdom literature. Think of it as a post-credits scene in your favorite blockbuster – a teaser for the sequels and spin-offs awaiting your exploration.

So, fellow time-travelers, as we launch the final chapter and gaze into the horizon, remember that Ecclesiastes isn't just a book; it's an invitation to embark on a timeless quest for understanding. It's not confined to the dusty archives of antiquity; it's a living, breathing guide for the cosmic explorers of today.

As you traverse the landscape of Ecclesiastes, may its wisdom be your guiding star through the time-traveling odyssey of existence. And as you reach the final chapter, the curtain call, carry this ancient wisdom in your time-traveling backpack – a compass for navigating the uncharted territories of your journey.

Your Invitation!

As you crack open this literary time capsule, consider yourself equipped with a state-of-the-art DeLorean of the mind. Your destination? The past, present, and future of Ecclesiastes, where ancient scrolls meet 21st-century wit in a temporal mashup that's cooler than a polaroid snapshot.

This isn't your average journey. It's a rendezvous with sages, philosophers, and maybe a few witty time-traveling quips along the way. Think of yourself as a wisdom hunter, armed with the ultimate time-turner, ready to unravel the threads of existence woven into these pages.

As you flip through the chapters, imagine you're maneuvering through the gears of time, each page a wormhole into the thoughts of the ages. Ecclesiastes isn't just a book; it's a TARDIS, a time machine inviting you to explore the landscapes of life's meaning, human folly, and the pursuit of a purposeful existence.

So, fellow temporal explorer, don't just read – time-travel! Let Ecclesiastes be your trusty guide in this epic quest across the centuries. Will you encounter pearls of ancient wisdom or maybe a few witty paradoxes? The adventure begins as soon as you turn the first page.

Ready to warp into a world where the past, present, and future collide in a symphony of thought? The DeLorean awaits, and your ticket is the curiosity in your heart. As you dive in, remember: the only limit is your imagination, and in the vast expanse of the written word, time is but a flexible friend.

Let the time-traveling commence!

PS: Get Ready for Group Discussions

- Listen to others with love.

- Listen to others from your heart. Try to understand the heart of what others are sharing.

- Listen to others with a non-judgmental attitude. You may disagree, but you can affirm that person's right to a different point of view.

- Listen to others with respect for their freedom. The group does not exist to give advice, but to encourage growth. We do not have to be of one voice or one mind.

- Listen to others with shared trust. A basic level of trust encourages sharing beyond the superficial. All sharing must be kept confidential.

- Speak from your own experience. Use the pronoun "I" when you share your point of view.

Chapter 1: Ecclesiastes 1 - The Pursuit of Meaning in a Digital Age

As we set our temporal coordinates to delve into Ecclesiastes 1 – the pursuit of meaning in a digital age. Picture this chapter as our time-travel manual, a guide through the historical code of ancient wisdom, navigating through the digital epochs with the finesse of a seasoned time voyager.

In the vast expanse of Ecclesiastes 1, we embark on a journey akin to deciphering the rhythms of life's time-travelling mixtape. It's a perpetual dance between the dawn of new experiences and the dusk of fleeting moments, a symphony echoing through the corridors of time.

As we navigate the digital landscape, Ecclesiastes 1 challenges us to confront the illusions of self-portrayal – a timeless selfie where comparisons abound in an era adorned with pixelated filters and perfected images. Here, authenticity becomes our compass, guiding us through the ever-changing pixels of our narrative.

Join me in exploring the temporal responsibility embedded in Ecclesiastes 1 – a pledge to tread lightly through the epochs of our shared existence. It's a call to action, reminding us that even the smallest choices in our temporal journey can create ripples across the digital fabric of time.

Our temporal journey continues as we unravel the pursuit of meaning in a world fixated on accumulating temporal treasures. Ecclesiastes reflects on the hollowness of chasing material gains without finding true fulfillment, urging us to forge genuine connections amidst the dazzling allure of digital status symbols.

In Ecclesiastes 1, we confront temporal unpredictability – an invitation to a poker game where the cards are dealt with an unpredictable hand. In a temporal realm addicted to certainty and control, Ecclesiastes nudges us to embrace the unexpected, finding beauty in the temporal chaos that unfolds with each time jump and temporal shift.

So, fellow time-travelers, fasten your temporal seatbelts for an interstellar journey through Ecclesiastes 1, where the pursuit of meaning meets the algorithms of our digital age. Let the temporal insights of this ancient scroll guide you through the historical constellations of existence, reminding us that even in the glow of screens, the quest for meaning remains the ultimate adventure. Are you ready to decode the pixels and uncover the temporal significance woven into the digital tapestry of Ecclesiastes 1? Let the pursuit of meaning in the digital age commence!

The Cyclical Nature of Life

1:2 - "Everything is meaningless," says the Teacher, "completely meaningless!"

The author begins by expressing a weariness that transcends generations, capturing the universal sentiment that no matter how much we witness or experience, true satisfaction remains elusive. "Everything is wearisome beyond description. No matter how much we see, we are never satisfied. No matter how much we hear, we are not content." These words resonate across time, encapsulating the perennial quest for fulfillment that each generation undertakes.

1:4 - Generations come and generations go, but the earth never changes.

The acknowledgment of the cyclical rhythm of life unfolds as the author observes, "Generations come and generations go, but the earth never changes." This statement encapsulates the essence of cyclical existence, where the footsteps of ancestors echo in the present, and the cycle continues with each new generation.

1:5 - The rises and the sun sets, then hurries around to rise again.

The symbolism of the sun, rising and setting, becomes a poignant metaphor for the cyclical nature of life. "The sun rises and the sun sets then hurries around to rise again." This mirrors the repetitive patterns of our lives, emphasizing the cyclical nature inherent no matter what time we travel to.

1:15 - What is wrong cannot be made right. What is missing cannot be recovered.

Amidst the acknowledgment of cyclical patterns, Ecclesiastes challenges us to confront the limitations within these repetitions. "What is wrong cannot be made right. What is missing cannot be recovered." Here, the cyclicality is not just a passive observation but an invitation to grapple with the inherent limitations of our human endeavors, urging us to find purpose beyond the predictable cycles.

1:18 - The greater my wisdom, the greater my grief. To increase knowledge only increases sorrow.

The pursuit of knowledge and wisdom is also examined in the context of life's cyclical nature. "The greater my wisdom, the greater my grief. To increase knowledge only increases sorrow." This reflection suggests that even the pursuit of wisdom, a noble endeavor, is not exempt from the cyclicality of life, bringing both enlightenment and a heightened awareness of life's complexities.

In these selected verses from Ecclesiastes 1, the cyclical nature of life is portrayed as a profound and inescapable reality. The scripture invites readers to contemplate the recurring patterns, acknowledge the limitations, and find meaning within the cycles that define our journey through the vast expanse of time.

Technology and Digital Distractions.

Let's decrypt Ecclesiastes 1 for our digital escapade through the maze of technology and distractions. Picture Ecclesiastes as our ancient guide navigating the vast internet of existence, dropping wisdom nuggets like breadcrumbs through the epochs of ones and zeros.

In the digital realm, where the endless scroll rules, Ecclesiastes 1 reminds us, "Everything is wearisome beyond description in the digital realm. No matter how much we scroll, we are never satisfied. No matter how many cat videos we watch, we are not content." It's like a never-ending loop of online content – just when you think you've seen it all, a new meme emerges, and the cycle starts anew.

Generations may come and go, but the tech landscape remains. "New gadgets come, and old gadgets go, but the digital world never changes." The march of progress in the tech world mirrors the relentless flow of time. We might upgrade our devices, but the essence of the digital dance persists, much like an ever-evolving software running in the background.

As we bask in the glow of screens, Ecclesiastes 1 challenges us to confront the vanity of comparisons in the era of social media selfies. "The digital selfie reigns and fades away, then hurries around to trend again." It's an Instagram carousel of self-portrayal, where filters and hashtags create a virtual self that loops back into the feed, craving likes and validation in an ever-revolving cycle.

What's missing in our digital quest for meaning, Ecclesiastes wonders, cannot be recovered through endless scrolling. The algorithmic search doesn't hold the secrets to fulfillment. As we navigate through the digital wormholes, the pursuit of knowledge in the form of Wikipedia dives and TED Talk marathons might bring enlightenment but, Ecclesiastes warns, "The greater your digital wisdom, the greater your data grief. To increase digital knowledge only increases techno-sorrow." The more we know, the more we realize the vastness of what we don't know in this virtual universe.

So, in this time-traveling expedition through Ecclesiastes 1, let's heed the ancient advice while navigating the binary constellations of our digital odyssey. Remember, in the dance of technology, there's a call to find purpose beyond the pixelated loops. Ecclesiastes might not provide an app for meaning, but it certainly offers a timeless guide for our quest in this digital age.

Recognize the Patterns

Picture this: the gentle hum of notifications, the ebb and flow of emails, the perpetual scroll through timelines – these are the rhythms that orchestrate the symphony of our digital days. In recognizing the patterns, we become code-breakers.

Just as Ecclesiastes hinted at the cyclicality of life, our digital journey unveils its loops. The rise and fall of viral trends, the predictable cycles of content virality, the recurring themes in memes – these are the modern echoes of ancient patterns, woven into the fabric of our online existence.

Scroll through your social feeds, and you'll witness the connections – likes, comments, shares – all choreographed by algorithms. Recognizing these rhythms is akin to tapping into the heartbeat of our interconnected digital universe, where each interaction is a note in the grand symphony of virtual relationships.

Yet, in this digital age, we're not merely spectators of patterns; we're active participants. The content we create, and the conversations we engage in – contribute to the ongoing rhythm of the online ecosystem. Our digital footprints become steps in our modern-day life, leaving imprints on the timeline of the universe.

As we navigate the digital corridors, recognizing patterns is also about deciphering the signals amid the noise. Amidst the constant chatter of notifications and the flickering pixels of information, discerning meaningful patterns becomes an art. It's like finding constellations in the vast expanse of a digital night sky, where meaningful insights sparkle amidst the data-driven galaxies.

In recognizing the patterns and rhythms of life in the digital age, we become masters of our narratives. Whether it's the familiar pulse of a favorite podcast, the rhythmic exchange of messages with friends, or the predictable cycles of online trends, these patterns guide us through the labyrinth of our connected existence.

Discussion Questions

Here are some group discussion questions to explore how individuals can overcome the seemingly meaningless patterns of technological life using insights from Ecclesiastes 1:

Reflection on Digital Exhaustion:
How do you feel about the weariness described in Ecclesiastes 1 and its relevance to the constant engagement with technology?

Can you identify moments in your technological life where you've experienced dissatisfaction or fatigue?

Generations and Technological Change:
In what ways do you think Ecclesiastes' acknowledgment of generations coming and going applies to the rapid changes in technology?

How can recognizing the ongoing digital evolution help us find meaning amid constant technological shifts?

The Vanity of Digital Comparisons:
Ecclesiastes 1 touches on the vanity of comparisons. How can this wisdom be applied to the digital world, especially in the age of social media?

In what ways do online comparisons contribute to feelings of dissatisfaction and discontentment?

Seeking Authentic Connections in the Digital Selfie Era:
How can Ecclesiastes' reflection on the vanity of selfies relate to the digital self-portrayal on social media?

What steps can we take to seek more authentic connections in the digital realm amidst the pressure to present curated images of ourselves?

The Pursuit of Digital Knowledge and Wisdom:
Ecclesiastes suggests that increasing knowledge can lead to increased sorrow. How might this concept apply to our constant pursuit of digital information?

In what ways can we balance our quest for digital wisdom without succumbing to the potential drawbacks mentioned in Ecclesiastes?

Embracing the Unpredictability of Digital Life:
Ecclesiastes 1 discusses the unpredictability of life. How can this idea be applied to the uncertainties and surprises of our digital experiences?

Can embracing the unexpected aspects of digital life contribute to finding meaning in the ever-changing online landscape?

Balancing Screen Time and Authentic Experiences:
How do you manage the balance between digital engagement and real-life experiences?

Can Ecclesiastes' reflections on the cyclical nature of life prompt us to reconsider how we spend our time in the digital realm?

Purposeful Digital Interactions:
Ecclesiastes invites us to find purpose beyond repetitive cycles. How can we infuse purpose into our digital interactions?

What practices can be adopted to ensure that our digital engagements contribute to a meaningful narrative rather than falling into repetitive patterns?

Digital Detox and Reflection:
Have you ever considered a digital detox to break free from the wearisome patterns described in Ecclesiastes?

How might taking intentional breaks from technology contribute to a more meaningful and purposeful digital life?

Implementing Ecclesiastes' Wisdom in Technological Contexts:

How can we practically implement Ecclesiastes 1's wisdom in our daily technological interactions?

Can you share personal strategies or experiences where applying Ecclesiastes' insights has positively influenced your digital life?

These questions can serve as a starting point for meaningful discussions on how individuals and communities can navigate and find purpose in the digital age, drawing wisdom from Ecclesiastes 1.

Conclusion

As we're about to wrap up Chapter 1, my fellow time-travel pals, let's take a chill moment to think about the rollercoaster of digital life we've just surfed. Ecclesiastes 1 has been our tech-savvy guide, helping us decode the funky patterns in the digital universe.

We've cruised through the ups and downs of weariness, cracked the code of online rhythms, and faced the whole issue of selfie drama. But guess what? We're not hitting pause just yet; Chapter 2 is on the horizon, and it's all about the illusion of success. Buckle up, because we're about to dive into the world of promotions, LinkedIn hype, and the not-so-glamorous side of climbing the success ladder.

In the next chapter, Ecclesiastes is throwing us into a corporate maze. Is success as shiny as it seems, or are we just grinding on a never-ending treadmill? Get ready to uncover the real deal about success in the digital age – it's not always the flashy stuff you see on the gram.

As we time-jump into Chapter 2, keep in mind that success in our digital era might be more like a Snapchat filter than a legitimate achievement. It's time to see through the illusions, figure out what success means to you, and maybe even tweak the definition a bit.

So, my awesome time-travel buddies, as we say peace out to Chapter 1, let's rev our virtual engines for the mind-blowing discoveries waiting in Chapter 2. The adventure continues, and who knows what crazy twists are ahead? Until then, keep scrolling, keep vibing, and always stay one step ahead in this epic journey of existence!

Chapter 2: Ecclesiastes 2 - The Illusion of Success

We've strapped into our virtual DeLorean, and now we're gearing up to dissect what success means in this wild digital ride. Chapter 1 was like the warm-up playlist, getting us hyped for the main event. Now, Ecclesiastes is throwing us into the neon-lit hustle of the corporate labyrinth. Imagine it as a virtual reality game where success isn't just about levelling up; it's about figuring out if the whole game is rigged.

In this chapter, we're about to unmask the illusions that make success look like a glitzy Insta story. Ecclesiastes is our guide, dropping truth bombs about promotions, LinkedIn connections, and the whole illusionary shebang. We're not just talking about success; we're talking about the real deal, the behind-the-scenes action of climbing the success ladder in this digital age.

So, buckle up, fam. Chapter 2 is where we navigate through the smoke and mirrors of success. It's like trying to decode a TikTok dance – looks cool, but is it as legit as it seems? Ecclesiastes is challenging us to question the whole game, to see if we're on a genuine path to success or just chasing illusions.

As we dive into this chapter, keep your chill vibes intact. Success might look different for each of us, and Ecclesiastes is here to help us figure out what matters in this digital maze. Let's unravel the illusion of success and maybe even redefine what it means to win in this epic game of life. Ready or not, let's hit play on Chapter 2 and see what kind of illusions Ecclesiastes is about to drop on us!

Analyzing Ecclesiastes 2

Ecclesiastes 2 offers a profound exploration of success, achievement, and the pursuit of meaning, and its relevance in the context of the modern workplace is striking. Let's delve into key verses from Ecclesiastes 2 and analyze how they resonate with the pressures individuals face in the quest for success today.

2:4 - "I also tried to find meaning by building huge homes for myself and by planting beautiful vineyards."

In the pursuit of success, individuals may invest heavily in external markers like material wealth and luxurious lifestyles, believing they contribute to fulfillment and status.

2:11 - "But as I looked at everything, I had worked so hard to accomplish, it was all so meaningless—like chasing the wind. There was nothing really worthwhile anywhere."

Despite achieving professional milestones, the verse speaks to the potential emptiness felt when success is solely defined by external accomplishments, leaving individuals questioning the true worth of their efforts.

2:17 - "So I came to hate life because everything done here under the sun is so troubling. Everything is meaningless—like chasing the wind."

The pressure to continually achieve and meet societal expectations in the workplace can lead to frustration and a sense of meaninglessness if the pursuit lacks a deeper purpose.

2:24-25 - "So I decided there is nothing better than to enjoy food and drink and to find satisfaction in work. Then I realized that these pleasures are from the hand of God."

Ecclesiastes suggests finding satisfaction in work and enjoying life's pleasures, highlighting that genuine fulfillment may be found not just in achievement but also in the journey and the appreciation of God's gifts.

2:26 - "God gives wisdom, knowledge, and joy to those who please him. But if a sinner becomes wealthy, God takes the wealth away and gives it to those who please him."

The verse emphasizes the importance of aligning one's pursuits with ethical principles and suggests that true success and wisdom come to those who seek to please a higher purpose.

In the modern workplace, where success is often measured by tangible achievements and material gains, Ecclesiastes 2 invites individuals to critically examine the nature of their pursuits. It encourages a shift from purely external markers of success toward a holistic understanding that includes finding joy in work, appreciating life's simple pleasures, and aligning one's efforts with a deeper, more meaningful purpose. The timeless wisdom of Ecclesiastes 2 challenges the prevailing pressures for success and prompts reflection on the true sources of fulfillment and satisfaction in the complex dynamics of the contemporary workplace.

Worldly Success and Insights from Ecclesiastes

In Ecclesiastes 2, the quest for worldly success is laid bare, and drawing parallels between the book's insights and the relentless pursuit of achievement in the modern world unveils thought-provoking reflections.

Endless Pursuit of Pleasure (Ecclesiastes 2:4):

Book's Insight: The author explores the construction of grand homes and the planting of beautiful vineyards in the pursuit of pleasure.

Parallel to the Modern World: Today, the workplace often witnesses a parallel pursuit, where individuals relentlessly chase after material success, bigger homes, and a lavish lifestyle, believing these external markers equate to happiness and fulfillment.

Vanity of External Achievements (Ecclesiastes 2:11):

Book's Insight: Despite numerous accomplishments, the author declares these achievements as ultimately meaningless, akin to chasing the wind.

Parallel to the Modern World: The pressure to achieve external milestones – promotions, accolades, and financial success – echoes this sentiment. Individuals may find themselves questioning the true worth of their relentless pursuit when faced with the emptiness that can accompany such external validations.

Frustration in Labor (Ecclesiastes 2:17):

Book's Insight: The author expresses a deep frustration with life and work, finding it troubling and ultimately meaningless.

Parallel to the Modern World: The modern workplace, with its demanding expectations and continuous pursuit of success, can lead individuals to experience frustration and a sense of meaninglessness if the journey lacks intrinsic value and purpose.

Enjoyment of Work and Pleasures as a Gift (Ecclesiastes 2:24-25):

Book's Insight: The author suggests finding satisfaction in work and enjoying life's pleasures as gifts from the hand of God.

Parallel to the Modern World: Ecclesiastes encourages a shift from a purely achievement-focused mindset to one that values the enjoyment of work and life's simple pleasures. In the modern world, individuals may find fulfillment by appreciating the journey and acknowledging the value in both professional and personal aspects of life.

The Gift of Wisdom (Ecclesiastes 2:26):

Book's Insight: God gives wisdom, knowledge, and joy to those who please Him, highlighting the significance of aligning one's pursuits with higher principles.

Parallel to the Modern World: In the pursuit of success, the book's insight encourages individuals to seek wisdom and joy by aligning their endeavors with ethical and meaningful principles, suggesting that true success comes not just from personal gain but from contributing positively to a higher purpose.

Drawing parallels between Ecclesiastes 2 and the contemporary chase for worldly success prompts a critical examination of values and priorities. The book challenges the prevailing notion that external accomplishments alone lead to true fulfillment. In a world often driven by material success, Ecclesiastes invites individuals to consider a more holistic approach to success—one that encompasses the joy of the journey, the appreciation of life's simple pleasures, and the pursuit of wisdom aligned with higher principles. It is a timeless guide encouraging reflection on the authentic sources of satisfaction and purpose amid the clamor for worldly success.

Discovering Authentic Success Beyond Societal Expectations

Let's talk about finding success that's legit for us, not what society says is cool. Ecclesiastes is like the wise grandparent dropping truth bombs, saying success isn't just about ticking boxes on society's checklist. Here's the lowdown on discovering real success, beyond what everyone else thinks:

Flipping the Script:

Ecclesiastes is all about flipping the script on what success means. It's like telling us to ditch the pressure of meeting everyone else's expectations and look for success in our way.

Breaking Illusions:

Forget about the smoke and mirrors of society's success game. Ecclesiastes is like the ultimate debunker, showing us that success isn't just about flashy achievements. It's about keeping it real and questioning what we're chasing.

Enjoying the Ride:

Ecclesiastes wants us to vibe with the journey, not just the end game. It's like saying, "Hey, don't just grind for the result; enjoy the process, the ups, and the downs."

Valuing the Real Deal:

Beyond what's trending on Insta, Ecclesiastes is pushing us to value what's real. Success isn't just about impressing others; it's about doing stuff that matters to us.

Doing You with Integrity:

It's all about doing you authentically. Ecclesiastes is like your hype-person, cheering you on to align your moves with your values, creating a vibe that's true to you.

Your Definition, Your Rules:

Forget the cookie-cutter definition of success. Ecclesiastes is handing us the mic, saying, "Define success on your terms. It's your show, your rules."

Seeing the Big Picture:

Ecclesiastes is zooming out to the bigger picture. Success isn't just about the job title; it's about having a dope personal life, meaningful relationships, and feeling good inside.

Adding to the Bigger Story:

Real success isn't a solo gig. Ecclesiastes is nudging us to contribute to something bigger – whether it's a cause we care about, ethical moves, or just making the world a little better.

Balancing Hustle and Chill:

Ecclesiastes is the chill friend saying, "Go crush your goals, but don't forget to chill too." It's about finding that sweet spot between chasing dreams and appreciating what's happening now.

Ecclesiastes is dropping wisdom that's as relevant to us as the latest memes. It's like having an older sibling spill the tea on success: keep it real, do your thing, and enjoy the ride. Let's vibe with our version of success, because, honestly, we're the bosses of our own stories.

Discussion Questions
The Pursuit of Pleasure (Ecclesiastes 2:4-10):
How does the author describe the pursuit of pleasure, including the building of houses and planting vineyards?

In what ways do people today seek pleasure and leisure as a means of finding fulfillment?

The Vanity of Achievements (Ecclesiastes 2:11):
What is the author's perspective on the meaning and value of his achievements as he reflects on them?

How might this reflection relate to the modern tendency to measure success by external accomplishments?

Frustration in Labor (Ecclesiastes 2:17-23):
How does the author express frustration in his toil and labor?

Can you draw parallels between the author's frustrations and common sentiments in the modern workplace?

Finding Joy in Work and Pleasure (Ecclesiastes 2:24-26):
What shift in perspective does the author make regarding finding joy in work and pleasure?

How can this perspective be applied to contemporary attitudes towards work and finding satisfaction?

Chasing After Wisdom (Ecclesiastes 2:26):
How does the author connect God's gifts of wisdom, knowledge, and joy with those who please Him?

In a modern context, how might individuals seek wisdom and align their pursuits with ethical principles to find true success?

Balancing Ambition and Contentment:
How can individuals balance ambition and contentment in their personal and professional lives?

Can you think of examples where too much ambition or a lack of contentment affected someone's well-being?

Defining Personal Success:
According to Ecclesiastes 2, what elements contribute to a sense of personal success?

How might individuals today define personal success beyond external markers?

Aligning Work with Personal Values:
How important is it for individuals to align their work with personal values and principles?

Can you share examples of how aligning work with personal values contributes to a sense of purpose and fulfillment?

Coping with Frustration and Meaninglessness:
How do individuals cope with feelings of frustration and meaninglessness in their work or personal lives?

Are there modern practices or approaches that echo the strategies suggested or explored by the author in Ecclesiastes 2?

Contributing to a Higher Purpose:
How might individuals contribute to a higher purpose in their daily lives or careers?

Can you think of examples where people have found fulfillment by contributing to something beyond personal success?

These questions can spark insightful conversations about the timeless themes explored in Ecclesiastes Chapter 2 and their relevance to the challenges and aspirations of contemporary life.

Conclusion

Buckle up because we're wrapping up Chapter 2, and Chapter 3 is about to hit us with the real talk about consumerism and the endless chase. Ecclesiastes is like our OG mentor, spilling the tea on the hustle, and we're here for it. Let's vibe into this conclusion and get pumped for what's next!

So, we've been cruising through the illusions of success, questioning the whole grind, and now we're about to dive into the wild world of consumerism. Ecclesiastes got us thinking – is this endless chase for stuff and status really where it's at? Spoiler alert: we're about to find out.

As we close the curtains on Chapter 2, remember this isn't just a break; it's the intermission before we plunge into the next blockbuster. Picture it like scrolling through trailers, and now we're getting a sneak peek into Chapter 3 – the Consumerism Chronicles.

Consumerism, fam. It's like the Matrix trying to plug us into the never-ending chase for the latest and greatest. Ecclesiastes is gearing up to spill some truth bombs about whether all this stuff we're after really brings the satisfaction it promises. Get ready to question the hype, challenge the trends, and maybe rethink your wishlist.

And let's keep it real, Chapter 3 isn't just a lecture on budgeting; it's Ecclesiastes dropping wisdom that's as relevant to us as the hottest memes. So, squad, let's hit pause on the shopping carts, take a deep breath, and gear up for the next adventure. Ecclesiastes is about to guide us through the maze of consumerism, and we're here to soak in the lessons like the pros we are.

As we step into Chapter 3, remember – it's not just a chapter; it's a rollercoaster ride of insights. So, tighten those shoelaces, grab your metaphorical popcorn, and let's get ready for the thrill of unravelling the mysteries of consumerism with Ecclesiastes as our guide. It's going to be epic, and we're ready for the ride!

Chapter 3: Ecclesiastes 3 - Consumerism and the Endless Chase

Welcome to Chapter 3 – where Ecclesiastes is about to spill some major tea on consumerism and the never-ending chase for the next big thing. It's like our ancient guide dropping truth bombs about whether all this hype around stuff and status is worth it. So, grab your favorite snacks, because we're diving deep into the world of trends, splurges, and the relentless pursuit of more.

Picture this chapter as a reality check for the age of endless choices and online shopping. Ecclesiastes is about to be our unfiltered voice, questioning if all these material desires and the hype around them lead to the satisfaction they promise. It's not just about what's in your closet; it's about what's in your soul, you feel?

As 18-year-olds navigating a world that throws trends at us like confetti, we've all been there – the pressure to keep up, the FOMO, the rush of the latest gadget. But Ecclesiastes is here to guide us through the chaos, helping us separate the must-haves from the maybe-not-so-much.

So, let's kick off Chapter 3 like we're entering the VIP section of a party. Ecclesiastes is our backstage pass to peek behind the curtain of consumerism. It's time to question the endless chase, challenge the status quo, and maybe even redefine what it means to be satisfied.

As we dive into this chapter, keep it real, keep it you, and let's uncover the hidden truths behind the shiny facade of consumer culture. Ecclesiastes is our ancient mentor, but trust me, the wisdom it's about to drop is as relevant as the latest TikTok dance. So, fam, let's turn the page and get ready to decode the mysteries of consumerism like the savvy trendsetters we are!

Examining Ecclesiastes 3

Ecclesiastes 3 is a timeless exploration that resonates profoundly with the themes of consumerism and the relentless pursuit embedded in the modern era.

3:1-2 - "For everything, there is a season, a time for every activity under heaven. A time to be born and a time to die, a time to plant and a time to harvest."

These verses could be interpreted as cycles of consumerism – a time to acquire (be born), a time to discard (die), a time to desire (plant), and a time to attain (harvest). Consumerism operates in seasons of acquisition and disposal.

3:6-7 - "A time to search and a time to quit searching. A time to keep and a time to throw away. A time to tear and a time to mend. A time to be quiet and a time to speak."

The pursuit of material gain is depicted here, reflecting the constant cycle of seeking, acquiring, discarding, and the struggle between silence (contentment) and the need to proclaim (consume).

3:9-10 - "What do people really get for all their hard work? I have seen the burden God has placed on us all."

The endless chase is questioned, prompting reflection on the real rewards of incessant labor and material pursuit. It highlights the burden imposed by the constant desire for more.

3:12-13 - "So I concluded there is nothing better than to be happy and enjoy ourselves as long as we can. And people should eat and drink and enjoy the fruits of their labor, for these are gifts from God."

The verses underline the fleeting nature of material accumulation and highlight the importance of finding joy in life's simple pleasures, as opposed to an endless chase for more.

3:13-14 - "And people should eat and drink and enjoy the fruits of their labor, for these are gifts from God. And I know that whatever God does is final. Nothing can be added to it or taken from it. God's purpose is that people should fear him."

The verses suggest finding joy in the fruits of labor as gifts from God. It challenges the notion that the pursuit of material goods is the ultimate source of fulfillment and emphasizes the finality of God's purpose over the insatiable nature of consumerism.

3:22-23 - "So I saw that there is nothing better for people than to be happy in their work. That is our lot in life. And no one can bring us back to see what happens after we die."

Ecclesiastes acknowledges the pursuit of happiness in one's work but cautions against the illusion that acquiring more will bring ultimate satisfaction. It emphasizes the limitations of material pursuits in addressing the deeper questions of life.

In summary, Ecclesiastes 3, within the lens of consumerism and the endless chase, serves as a reflection on the cyclical nature of desire, acquisition, and the pursuit of satisfaction. It challenges the prevailing notions of fulfillment through material gain, urging individuals to find contentment in the simple joys of life and recognize the limitations of the never-ending chase for more.

Our Consumer-driven Culture

In the hustle and bustle of the 21st-century consumer-driven culture, Ecclesiastes 3 offers a profound guide to navigate the ever-churning cycle of desires and the relentless pursuit of material wealth. Let's explore how the wisdom from Ecclesiastes 3 can be applied to the challenges posed by modern consumerism:

Recognizing Seasons of Consumption:

Ecclesiastes 3 prompts us to recognize the seasons of consumption – there's a time to acquire and a time to let go. In a culture constantly bombarding us with new products and trends, wisdom lies in discerning when to embrace the novelty and when to release the burden of excessive possessions.

Embracing Contentment:

The pursuit of material wealth often leads to a perpetual chase, yet Ecclesiastes advocates for contentment. In a society that glorifies the accumulation of possessions, the wisdom of Ecclesiastes invites individuals to find satisfaction in the present, appreciating what they have rather than relentlessly seeking more.

Balancing Work and Enjoyment:

Ecclesiastes 3 encourages us to balance our pursuit of material wealth with the enjoyment of life's simple pleasures. In a consumer-driven culture, the relentless focus on career and acquisition can overshadow the importance of savoring the fruits of our labor and finding joy in everyday moments.

Questioning the Endless Pursuit:

The book challenges the notion that endless material pursuit is the key to a fulfilling life. In a consumer-driven society that often equates success with the accumulation of possessions, Ecclesiastes encourages individuals to question whether this pursuit truly brings lasting satisfaction or if it's an endless loop leading to emptiness.

Appreciating the Gift of Now:

Ecclesiastes reminds us that the enjoyment of life's gifts is a present from the divine. In a world fixated on the next big purchase or trend, applying this wisdom means learning to appreciate the blessings of the current moment and finding joy in the simple yet precious aspects of life.

Balancing Material Desires with Spiritual Fulfillment:

The wisdom of Ecclesiastes encourages a balance between material desires and spiritual fulfillment. In a culture that often measures success solely by material wealth, applying this wisdom means recognizing the intrinsic value of spiritual and emotional well-being over the accumulation of possessions.

Reflecting on the True Value of Work:

Ecclesiastes prompts a reflection on the true value of work. In a consumer-driven culture that often ties personal worth to professional achievements and financial success, applying this wisdom involves understanding that genuine fulfillment comes not just from the work itself but from a harmonious balance with other aspects of life.

Cultivating Gratitude:

Ecclesiastes encourages a mindset of gratitude. Amid a culture that constantly fuels desires for the next big thing, applying this wisdom involves cultivating gratitude for what one has, fostering contentment in the face of societal pressures to always crave more.

In essence, Ecclesiastes 3 provides a timeless guide for individuals caught in the whirlwind of a consumer-driven culture. It urges a recalibration of values, inviting people to find contentment in the present, strike a balance between material pursuits and spiritual well-being, and question the assumptions of an endless chase for material wealth. Applying this wisdom allows individuals to navigate the complexities of modern consumerism with a deeper understanding of what truly brings meaning and satisfaction to their lives.

Finding Contentment

Ecclesiastes is dropping some wisdom for our journey through the ages. Imagine we're navigating through the time stream, and Ecclesiastes is the ultimate guide, telling us how to find that sweet spot in the ebb and flow of history. Let's break it down like time-traveling pros:

Riding Time's Waves:

Life is like a time wave, right? Ecclesiastes gets that there's a moment for everything – highs, lows, and all the timelines in between. It's like saying, "Sometimes you're in the time vortex, and other times, it's a pause. That's just the time playlist, so ride the waves!"

Chilling in the Present Epoch:

Ecclesiastes is all about soaking up the present epoch. In a world that's constantly pushing us to think about the next era, it's like a reminder to hit the pause button, enjoy the timeline you're on, and be grateful for the beats of now.

Flexing with the Temporal Seasons:

Life's got temporal seasons – not just weather-wise, but in every era. Ecclesiastes says it's cool to flex with these temporal seasons. Sometimes you're in hustle mode, and other times, it's time travel and chill. Embracing the temporal seasons means less stress and more timey-winey flow.

No FOMO, Just JOTD:

Ecclesiastes is dropping major JOTD vibes – Joy of Timey Discoveries. It's like saying, "You don't have to be everywhere, experience every era. Enjoy where you're at without stressing about what you're missing." Less FOMO, more JOTD, you feel?

Balancing Time Hustle and Chill:

Life's a mixtape of time hustle and chill. Ecclesiastes gets it. It's saying, "Sure, grind for your temporal goals, but don't forget to kick back and enjoy the timelines too." Balancing the time hustle with some chill moments keeps the chrono-vibes in check.

Letting Go of the Uncontrollable Time Rifts:

Ecclesiastes vibes with the idea of letting go of what we can't control across time rifts. Some things are like unpredictable time shifts – you can't control 'em. So, chill, ride it out, and focus on what you can traverse instead of stressing about the untamed temporal currents.

Appreciating the Beats of Timelines:

Ecclesiastes invites us to appreciate the beats of timelines. Life's a playlist, and each historical moment is a track. Whether it's a bop or a slow jam, finding contentment is about grooving to the beats and appreciating the diversity of the historical tunes life throws at you.

Rolling with the Temporal Flow:

Life is part of a temporal dance, according to Ecclesiastes. It's like saying, "Roll with the temporal flow." Recognize that you're a part of something bigger across timelines, and finding contentment is about syncing up with the rhythm of the temporal currents.

Ecclesiastes is the temporal guide telling us to chill, ride the waves through history, and enjoy the soundtrack of our time-travelling adventures. It's the ultimate guide to finding contentment in the ebb and flow of the historical mixtape.

Discussion Questions:

Reflecting on Desires:

What are some desires or material possessions that you currently feel are crucial for your happiness?

How have these desires been influenced by societal expectations or consumer-driven culture?

Defining Contentment:

How would you personally define contentment in a world that often measures success by material possessions?

Do you believe contentment is a constant state, or can it be achieved through moments of satisfaction?

Gratitude Exercise:
Take a moment to list three things you're grateful for that aren't related to material possessions. How do these non-material aspects contribute to your well-being?

Balancing Ambition and Contentment:
How do you currently balance your ambitions and desire for success with finding contentment in the present moment?

Are there specific practices or mindsets you adopt to maintain this balance?

Experience Over Possessions:
Share an experience in your life that brought you more joy or contentment than any material possession. What made that experience special for you?

Social Media Influence:
Discuss the impact of social media on your perception of contentment. How does seeing others' lifestyles on platforms like Instagram influence your desires?

Activities:
Gratitude Journal:
Start a gratitude journal where you write down three things you're grateful for each day. Focus on non-material aspects to shift the focus away from possessions.

Digital Detox Day:
Plan a day where you disconnect from social media and technology. Spend the day engaging in activities that bring joy without relying on material distractions.

Community Volunteering:
Engage in a volunteer activity within your community. Reflect on how contributing to others' well-being can bring a sense of contentment beyond material pursuits.

Mindfulness Meditation:
Practice mindfulness meditation to center your thoughts on the present moment. Explore guided meditations that emphasize gratitude and contentment.

Swap and Share Event:
Organize a community swap event where individuals can exchange items they no longer need. This promotes a sense of community, and sustainability, and reduces the emphasis on constant consumption.

Minimalism Challenge:
Take part in a minimalism challenge where, for a set period, you intentionally reduce the number of material possessions. Reflect on how this impacts your overall sense of contentment.

Book Club Discussion:
Choose a book or article related to minimalism, gratitude, or finding contentment in non-material aspects. Discuss the key takeaways and how you can apply these principles in your life.

Nature Retreat:
Plan a nature retreat or hike. Spend time immersed in the outdoors and reflect on the simplicity and beauty of nature as a source of contentment.

These discussion questions and activities aim to encourage introspection, mindfulness, and a shift in focus from material possessions to experiences and values that contribute to a more content and fulfilled life.

Conclusion
Alright, trendsetters, as we wrap up Chapter 3 and gear up for Chapter 4, get ready to dive deep into the digital cosmos of social media. Ecclesiastes has been our guide through the ebb and flow of consumerism, and now we're about to tackle the vortex of comparisons and digital illusions.

So, here's the lowdown as we bid adieu to Chapter 3: Life's been a wild ride, full of temporal seasons, and Ecclesiastes has been the ultimate time-travelling mentor, teaching us how to find contentment in the historical mixtape.

But, hold tight, because Chapter 4 is about to hit us with a reality check on social media and the vanity of comparisons. In a world where Instagram filters and Snapchat streaks dominate, Ecclesiastes is here to drop some wisdom bombs about the true value of authenticity in a digital age.

As we close the digital chapter, remember – your worth isn't determined by likes, follows, or the comparison game. Ecclesiastes is inviting us to step back from the digital noise, embrace our unique timelines, and find contentment beyond the curated snapshots of others.

So, buckle up for Chapter 4 – the Social Media Saga. Ecclesiastes is about to challenge the illusions of perfection, question the value of digital status, and guide us through the maze of virtual comparisons. It's time to navigate the digital waves with wisdom, authenticity, and a dash of rebellious spirit.

As we launch into the realm of social media, let's keep in mind that Ecclesiastes isn't just a dusty old guide; it's a timeless mentor for the challenges of every era. So, crew, get ready to decode the digital matrix, and may your timelines be filled with genuine connections and authentic vibes.

Chapter 4, here we come – let's uncover the truths hidden behind the filters, and remember, the most authentic version of yourself is always trending.

Chapter 4: Ecclesiastes 4 - Social Media and the Vanity of Comparisons

Welcome to Chapter 4 – the realm of Social Media and the wild ride of comparisons. Ecclesiastes has been our time-travelling companion, guiding us through the highs and lows of the historical mixtape. Now, we're stepping into the matrix of likes, shares, and the illusionary world of social media.

So, picture this chapter as the ultimate reality check in a universe dominated by Instagram filters and viral tweets. Ecclesiastes is about to spill the tea on the vanity of comparisons and the digital game of illusions. Get ready for a journey that goes beyond the pixels, hashtags, and curated timelines.

We know the struggle – the pressure to measure up, the FOMO from everyone else's highlight reel. Ecclesiastes is our OG guide, about uncovering the secrets behind flawless profiles and challenging the value of digital status.

In this chapter, we're diving into the rabbit hole of social media. Ecclesiastes isn't here to rain on the selfie parade but to reveal the power of authenticity in a world often blinded by digital illusions. So, grab your smartphones, brace for impact, and let's navigate the digital maze with wisdom, wit, and a touch of rebellious spirit.

Chapter 4 is the Social Media Saga, and Ecclesiastes is about to teach us on the art of staying true in the age of comparisons. It's time to flip the script, question the curated narratives, and find contentment beyond the metrics. Are you ready to decode the matrix? Let's do this!

Ecclesiastes 4

Ecclesiastes 4, when analyzed through the lens of the Bible, offers insights into the dynamics of comparisons and their relevance to the digital age, particularly in the context of social media.

4:4 - "Then I observed that most people are motivated to succeed because they envy their neighbors. But this, too, is meaningless—like chasing the wind."

This verse highlights the prevalent motivation for success: envy of others. In the realm of social media, where curated content often portrays idealized versions of others' lives, the pursuit of success driven by comparison can lead to a sense of meaninglessness.

4:7-8 - "I observed yet another example of something meaningless under the sun. This is the case of a man who is all alone, without a child or a brother, yet who works hard to gain as much wealth as he can. But then he asks himself, 'Who am I working for? Why am I giving up so much pleasure now?' It is all so meaningless and depressing."

In the digital age, social media can contribute to the sense of isolation and comparison. Individuals may strive for wealth, popularity, or recognition, but the constant comparison to others' seemingly perfect lives can lead to a sense of futility and emptiness.

4:9-10 - "Two people are better off than one, for they can help each other succeed. If one person falls, the other can reach out and help. But someone who falls alone is in real trouble."

These verses emphasize the value of companionship and collaboration. In the context of social media, where individuals often compare their achievements and relationships, Ecclesiastes suggests that true success is found in genuine connections and mutual support.

4:13-14 - "It is better to be a poor but wise youth than an old and foolish king who refuses all advice. Such a youth could rise from poverty and succeed. He might even become king, though he has been in prison."

These verses challenge the conventional pursuit of status and success. In the digital age, where social media metrics can define one's perceived worth, Ecclesiastes suggests that wisdom and authenticity hold more value than the pursuit of popularity or conformity.

In summary, Ecclesiastes 4 provides a timeless reflection on the futility of comparisons driven by envy and the pursuit of success for its own sake. In the context of social media, these insights encourage individuals to seek authentic connections, find value in wisdom over popularity, and recognize the emptiness of a life driven solely by comparison.

The Impact of Social Media

Ecclesiastes 4 offers profound insights that resonate with the impact of social media on self-esteem and identity in the 21st century. Let's explore the parallels between the wisdom from Ecclesiastes 4 and the digital landscape:

Comparison and Envy:

Ecclesiastes 4:4 acknowledges that the pursuit of success often stems from envy and comparison. In the realm of social media, the constant exposure to curated, idealized versions of others' lives can trigger feelings of inadequacy and a relentless drive for validation.

Isolation and Loneliness:

Verses 7-8 speak to the emptiness of a life lived solely for personal gain without meaningful connections. In the age of social media, individuals may accumulate virtual friends and followers, yet experience a profound sense of isolation and loneliness, as digital interactions often lack depth and authenticity.

Mutual Support and Collaboration:

Ecclesiastes 4:9-12 extols the value of collaboration and mutual support. In contrast, social media platforms can sometimes foster unhealthy competition. However, these verses encourage us to seek genuine connections, where mutual encouragement and support contribute to a healthier self-esteem.

Authenticity over Popularity:

Verses 13-16 highlight the superiority of wisdom and authenticity over the pursuit of popularity and conformity. In the digital age, where social media metrics can define one's perceived worth, Ecclesiastes urges individuals to prioritize authenticity over conforming to societal or online expectations.

The Impact on Self-Esteem:

The overall message of Ecclesiastes 4 aligns with the impact of social media on self-esteem. The constant comparison, pursuit of external validation, and isolation from authentic connections can lead to a diminished sense of self-worth.

The Quest for Identity:

Ecclesiastes encourages individuals to find meaning beyond societal expectations and the pursuit of popularity. Similarly, in the digital age, where social media can shape perceptions of identity, Ecclesiastes prompts a reflection on finding one's true identity beyond the online persona.

In drawing parallels between Ecclesiastes 4 and the impact of social media on self-esteem and identity, the timeless wisdom encourages a shift in perspective. It calls for prioritizing genuine connections, embracing authenticity, and recognizing the limitations of a life driven solely by comparisons and the pursuit of digital acclaim. Ecclesiastes offers a guide to navigating the complexities of the digital landscape with wisdom and a focus on building a resilient and authentic sense of self.

Cultivating Genuine Connections

Let's talk real for a sec. In this wild, virtual jungle we call the internet, finding genuine connections might seem like trying to spot a unicorn. But guess what? It's doable, and it doesn't involve mastering some ancient online sorcery. Here's the lowdown on cultivating real connections in our digital playground:

Ditch the Filters:

Just like on Insta, life is better without filters. Be you, unapologetically. Embrace the quirks, the imperfections, and all the funky stuff that makes you, well, you. Authenticity is like a catnip for genuine connections.

Slide into the DMs (Politely):

Don't be afraid to shoot your shot, but let's keep it classy. Slide into those DMs with respect and genuine interest. Ask about their day, share a meme, or drop a compliment. Remember, we're here to build connections, not collect trophies.

Share the Real Stuff:

Virtual connections level up when you go beyond surface-level chit-chat. Share your passions, your fears, your latest Netflix binge – whatever makes you tick. Vulnerability creates a bond stronger than any Wi-Fi signal.

Emoji Game Strong:

Emojis are like the secret sauce of online convos. Use them wisely to add flavor to your messages. They're like the virtual version of body language – a smiley can turn a 'k' into a 'cool, let's chat more.'

Join the Community Vibe:

Dive into online communities that align with your interests. Whether it's a gaming group, a book club, or a meme haven, being part of a virtual crew gives you the chance to vibe with like-minded peeps.

Be a Good Listener (Read: Reader):

Genuine connections aren't just about talking; they're about listening. Read those messages, catch the vibes, and respond thoughtfully. Show that you're not just there for the LOLs but for the real talks too.

Plan IRL Hangouts:

Virtual connections can go IRL! Plan meet-ups, Zoom parties, or game nights. Turning pixels into real faces strengthens the connection game, and it's an epic way to create memories beyond the virtual realm.

Respect Boundaries:

Remember, not everyone is on the same connection wavelength. Respect boundaries, and if someone needs space, give it. Building genuine connections is a marathon, not a sprint.

So, there you have it – the ultimate guide to cultivating genuine connections in our virtual playground. It's all about keeping it real, being yourself, and sprinkling a bit of emoji magic. Now, go forth and create those epic virtual connections!

Discussion Questions:

Comparison Culture:

How has social media influenced your perceptions of success and happiness through the lens of others' posts?

In what ways do you find yourself comparing your life to what you see on social media?

Authenticity in a Digital World:
How can individuals maintain authenticity in the digital age where social media often encourages curated and idealized representations?

Share a personal experience where authenticity on social media positively impacted your connection with others.

Impact on Self-Esteem:
Discuss the potential impact of social media on self-esteem. How do likes, comments, or follower counts contribute to one's sense of self-worth?

Have you ever experienced a moment where social media negatively affected your self-esteem? How did you navigate it?

Navigating Digital Comparison:
What strategies do you use to avoid falling into the comparison trap on social media?

How can individuals encourage a culture of support and encouragement rather than competition on digital platforms?

Real vs. Virtual Connections:
Reflect on the differences between real-life connections and virtual connections on social media. In what ways can online relationships be as meaningful as offline ones?

Activities:
Digital Detox Day:
Challenge yourself and your friends to a digital detox day. Spend 24 hours without engaging in social media. Reflect on the experience and its impact on your mood and well-being.

#AuthenticChallenge:
Create a challenge within your social circle to share something authentic and unfiltered on social media. It could be a photo, a story, or a reflection that goes beyond the usual curated content.

Digital Journaling:
Start a digital journal where you document your feelings and experiences related to social media. Reflect on how your emotions change based on your online interactions.

Virtual Support Group:
Form a virtual support group with friends or online acquaintances. Discuss challenges related to social media, share tips on navigating comparison, and encourage one another.

Social Media Workshop:
Organize a workshop or discussion forum to share strategies for maintaining mental health and well-being in the age of social media. Invite guest speakers or experts to provide insights.

Offline Hangout:
Plan an offline hangout or activity with friends from your online circle. It could be a picnic, a game night, or a simple coffee meetup. Strengthening virtual connections in person can be a powerful experience.

Positive Content Challenge:
Challenge yourself and your online friends to share positive and uplifting content for a week. Focus on creating a supportive digital environment rather than contributing to negativity.

Reflection Session:
Set aside time for a group reflection session. Discuss any revelations or changes in perspective that occurred during the chapter's exploration of social media and comparisons.

These discussion questions and activities aim to foster thoughtful conversations about the impact of social media on individuals' well-being and encourage positive digital interactions.

Conclusion

We've just survived the wild ride of Chapter 4 – the Social Media Saga. We've unmasked the illusions, navigated the comparisons, and hopefully, you've kept your authenticity game strong. But guess what? Our journey is far from over. Buckle up because Chapter 5 is about to hit us with a different vibe – the Environment and Stewardship edition.

As we bid adieu to the likes, shares, and stories of Chapter 4, let's remember that the digital world is a place of both wonder and responsibility. It's like having a superpower – the power to influence, create change, and spread positive vibes. But, with great power comes great responsibility, right?

Now, we're stepping into Chapter 5 – the Green Zone. Ecclesiastes is gearing up to talk about our home, the planet Earth, and how we can be the ultimate stewards of this rad environment. It's not just about saving trees or picking up trash; it's about recognizing that our choices in the digital realm also impact the world beyond our screens.

So, get ready to swap out your digital gloves for eco-friendly ones. Ecclesiastes is about to drop wisdom bombs on being kick-butt stewards of our planet. Think of it as levelling up from social media influencers to Earth influencers. It's about understanding that every click, every post, has a ripple effect on the cosmic home we all share.

As we dive into Chapter 5, let's make a pact to be digital warriors with a cause. Ecclesiastes is challenging us to be the change-makers, the guardians of the environment, and to rock the digital world with a green heart. So, grab your virtual watering cans, plant some digital trees, and let's make this digital world an epic place for us and generations to come.

Chapter 5 – The Green Zone awaits, and we're about to embark on a journey of environmental stewardship like never before. It's time to turn the digital stage into a green oasis.

Chapter 5: Ecclesiastes 5 - The Environment and Stewardship: A Call to Responsible Living

Earth Protectors! Chapter 5 is rolling in like a boss, and guess what's on the menu? The Environment and Stewardship, aka the Green Zone. Ecclesiastes is about to spill the eco-tea, and we're all invited to the party. Get ready for a digital journey that's not just about pixels but also about saving the planet. Let's dive in with all the zest of an avocado-toast-loving, eco-warrior generation.

Now, I know what you're thinking – "Stewardship, what's that, some ancient term from the land before Wi-Fi?" Nope, it's not a spell from a fantasy novel; it's the key to being the ultimate Earth influencer. In this chapter, Ecclesiastes is throwing down the gauntlet, challenging us to be digital stewards, the eco-champions of the virtual cosmos.

Think of it like this: We've got the power to change the game, not just in our screensavers but in the real world. It's time to go from scrolling to strolling in nature, from digital likes to real-life green thumbs. Ecclesiastes is the OG mentor, showing us that every online choice we make has an impact on the planet we call home.

So, as we hit play on Chapter 5, let's rock our digital spaces with a green twist. Ecclesiastes isn't just preaching; it's inviting us to be the guardians of our cosmic home. It's about making sustainability cool, turning our virtual stage into a green haven, and proving that our generation is more than just memes and selfies – we're the Earth's digital allies.

Chapter 5 – The Green Zone – is our chance to be the eco-heroes we were born to be. So, grab your reusable water bottle, plant some virtual trees, and let's make this digital era a green revolution.

Connecting Ecclesiastes 5 with Contemporary Environmental Concerns

Ecclesiastes 5, when viewed through the lens of contemporary environmental concerns, offers profound insights that resonate with the challenges and responsibilities we face in safeguarding our planet. Let's explore key verses and draw connections to present-day environmental issues:

5:1 -"As you enter the house of God, keep your ears open and your mouth shut. It is evil to make mindless offerings to God."

In the context of environmental concerns, this verse encourages us to be attentive listeners to the needs of the Earth. Mindful actions, rather than thoughtless offerings, are crucial in addressing contemporary environmental challenges.

5:10 - "Those who love money will never have enough. How meaningless to think that wealth brings true happiness!"

The pursuit of wealth often leads to overconsumption and environmental degradation. This verse prompts reflection on the consequences of prioritizing material gain over the well-being of the planet.

5:11 - "The more you have, the more people come to help you spend it. So, what good is wealth—except perhaps to watch it slip through your fingers!"

Excessive consumption and resource exploitation are highlighted here, emphasizing the transient nature of material wealth. This echoes concerns about unsustainable resource usage in our modern society.

5:18 - "Even so, I have noticed one thing, at least, that is good. It is good for people to eat, drink, and enjoy their work under the sun during the short life God has given them, and to accept their lot in life."

While promoting the enjoyment of life, this verse also advocates for a balanced and sustainable approach. It encourages an appreciation for the Earth's resources without exploiting them to the point of environmental harm.

5:19 - "And it is a good thing to receive wealth from God and the good health to enjoy it. To enjoy your work and accept your lot in life—this is indeed a gift from God."

This verse suggests that the blessings of wealth and health come with the responsibility to steward them wisely. In the context of environmental concerns, it encourages a sense of gratitude for the Earth's resources and a commitment to preserving them for future generations.

5:20 - "God keeps such people so busy enjoying life that they take no time to brood over the past."

The emphasis on enjoying life without dwelling on the past aligns with the urgency of addressing contemporary environmental challenges. It encourages a forward-looking approach focused on sustainable practices.

In summary, Ecclesiastes 5, provides timeless wisdom applicable to contemporary environmental concerns. The verses call for mindful and balanced living, caution against unchecked materialism, and encourage responsible stewardship of the Earth's resources. These insights serve as a guide for fostering a sustainable and harmonious relationship with the environment in our modern world.

Encouraging a Sense of Responsibility

So, you've mastered the art of scrolling and liking, but have you ever thought about your digital carbon footprint? It's time to talk stewardship – not the kind with capes and castles but the real deal, where we become the guardians of our planet. Get ready for some eco-awesomeness, tailored just for you!

1. Rock the Green Lifestyle:

From reusable water bottles to saying no to fast fashion, small changes can make an impact. Show Mother Earth some love by adopting a green lifestyle. It's like giving your favorite influencer a follow, but way cooler.

2. Be a Digital Eco-Warrior:

Your digital playground is part of the Earth too. Unplug when you can, recycle your old gadgets, and think twice before hitting that print button. Being a digital eco-warrior is about making smart choices online, where every click counts.

3. Plant Virtual Trees, for Real:

Virtual trees may not grow in your backyard, but they sure can in your heart. Support eco-friendly apps and initiatives that plant real trees for your virtual actions. It's like turning your gaming skills into a forest of awesomeness.

4. Embrace the Power of Influence:

You don't need a million followers to be an influencer. Share your eco-journey on social media. Post about sustainable swaps, eco-friendly hacks, or your latest thrift store finds. Who knows, you might inspire your digital crew to join the green revolution.

5. Nature is Your Playground:
Stewardship is about falling in love with nature, not just double-tapping its pictures. Get outdoors, explore hiking trails, or organize a beach cleanup with your friends. Being hands-on with the environment makes you a true steward of the planet.

6. Dive into Sustainable Trends:
Who says sustainable isn't stylish? Dive into the world of eco-fashion, zero waste, and upcycling. Show off your unique style while keeping the planet in mind. It's like curating your wardrobe with a touch of Mother Nature's magic.

7. Spread the Green Vibes:
Stewardship is contagious – the more, the greener. Talk about it with your friends, start an eco-club at school, or organize virtual events that raise awareness about environmental issues. Your voice can be the catalyst for a green movement.

8. Educate, Don't Hesitate:
Share your knowledge about environmental issues. Create fun and engaging content that educates without preaching. Whether it's through memes, vlogs, or Insta stories, your voice matters in spreading the word about our shared responsibility for the planet.
Stewardship is not just a fancy word; it's a vibe, a lifestyle, and a commitment to making our world a better place. Let's be the generation that rocks the green, the ones who turn the tide and leave a legacy of love for Mother Earth.

Recognizing the Interconnectedness of Human Actions and the Environment
Let's talk about a mind-blowing concept: the interconnectedness of everything – yes, everything. You know that feeling when you drop a pebble into a pond, and ripples spread out? Well, imagine our actions as those ripples, reaching far and wide, not just on the surface but deep down into the roots of our existence. Here's the scoop on recognizing how every move we make is important to the environment.
1. The Ripple Effect:
Ever noticed how one decision can set off a chain reaction? It's like deciding to use a reusable water bottle – seems small, but the ripple effect is huge. Less plastic, less pollution, and that's just the beginning. Recognize the power in your choices; they're like ripples shaping the world around you.

2. From Farm to Fork:
What's on your plate is not just about your taste buds; it's a statement. Our food choices are deeply connected to the environment. Opting for local, seasonal, and sustainable eats isn't just a trend; it's a nod towards the positive with what we consume and the health of the planet.

3. Fashion Footprints:
Your fashion choices aren't just about looking fly; they leave footprints on the Earth. Fast fashion may be cheap, but its environmental cost is high. Embrace slow fashion, recycle your threads, and recognize that every outfit has a story – let yours be one of sustainability.

4. Energy Dance:

Flip a switch, and boom – lights on! But where does that power come from? Fossil fuels or renewable energy? Recognizing the source of our energy is like choosing the rhythm of our dance with the environment. Opt for renewables, and let your moves be in sync with a greener beat.

5. Digital Footprint Funk:

You're not just scrolling; you're leaving a digital footprint. From the energy used to power data centers to the materials in your gadgets, every online move has an environmental vibe. Be mindful; it's like choreographing a dance that respects the Earth's rhythm.

6. Waste Waltz:

Trash talk alert! Where does your waste end up doing its tango? Landfills or recycling centers? Recognize that our waste dance affects the environment's harmony. Reduce, reuse, and recycle – let's make waste management a graceful ballet.

7. Breathe Easy Ballet:

The air we breathe is a dance partner we can't live without. Recognize the impact of air pollution on our shared choreography. Supporting clean air initiatives, reducing emissions, and embracing green transportation are steps in the right direction.

8. Wildlife Waltz:

The creatures sharing this planet are part of our grand dance. Recognize the impact of human actions on biodiversity. Conservation efforts, responsible tourism, and preserving natural habitats – let's dance in a way that respects every participant in this cosmic ballet.

Recognizing the interconnectedness of our actions and the environment is like grooving to the most epic playlist of all time. Every move counts, and every decision shapes the dance. Let's be mindful dancers, choreographing a future where our steps leave a legacy of harmony, not chaos.

Discussion Questions
Ecclesiastes 5 and its potential implications for environmental stewardship:
Reflection on Materialism:
How does Ecclesiastes 5:10, "Those who love money will never have enough," relate to our modern consumer-driven society and its impact on the environment?

Stewardship and Wealth:
Ecclesiastes 5 emphasizes being content with what one has. How can adopting a mindset of contentment influence our ecological footprint and reduce the environmental strain caused by overconsumption?

Environmental Impact of Wealth Pursuit:
Considering Ecclesiastes 5:11, "The more you have, the more people come to help you spend it," how might the pursuit of wealth contribute to environmental issues, such as resource depletion and pollution?

Balancing Enjoyment and Responsibility:
Ecclesiastes 5:18 encourages enjoying life but also accepting one's lot. How can we balance the enjoyment of the Earth's resources with the responsibility to protect and preserve the environment for future generations?

Consumer Choices and Environmental Consequences:
How do Ecclesiastes 5:19, "And it is a good thing to receive wealth from God and the good health to enjoy it," prompt us to consider the environmental consequences of our lifestyle choices, especially in terms of consumption and waste?

Impact of Mindful Choices on the Environment:
How can the concept of mindfulness, as suggested in Ecclesiastes 5:1 ("As you enter the house of God, keep your ears open and your mouth shut"), be applied to our environmental choices, such as reducing waste, choosing sustainable products, and supporting eco-friendly initiatives?

Appreciating Nature's Gifts:
Ecclesiastes 5:19 speaks of wealth and good health as gifts from God. In what ways can we appreciate the Earth's resources as gifts and, in turn, be inspired to steward them responsibly?

Wealth and Climate Responsibility:
In the context of Ecclesiastes 5, how might the pursuit of wealth align with or diverge from our responsibility to address climate change and other environmental challenges?

Balancing Progress and Environmental Impact:
Ecclesiastes 5 encourages us to enjoy our work but also accept our lot. How can this wisdom guide our approach to technological advancements and industrial progress, ensuring they align with environmental sustainability?

Practical Steps for Environmental Stewardship:
Drawing insights from Ecclesiastes 5, what practical steps can individuals take to be better stewards of the environment in their daily lives?

These discussion questions aim to explore the relevance of Ecclesiastes 5 in the context of environmental stewardship and encourage thoughtful reflections on how biblical wisdom can guide our actions in addressing contemporary environmental challenges.

Conclusion

We've just rocked Chapter 5 – The Green Zone. We've explored the wonders of environmental stewardship and investigated the landscape of our shared planet. But guess what? Our journey continues, and Chapter 6 is about to drop – brace yourselves for Relationships in the Digital Age.

As we bid farewell to the virtual trees we've planted, the sustainable choices we've made, and the eco-warrior vibes we've embraced, let's keep the momentum going. Chapter 6 isn't just about swiping left or right; it's a deep dive into the intricate connections in the digital era.

So, put on your digital armor, charge up your empathy circuits, and get ready for a journey through the realms of friendships, romances, and the tangled web of social networks. Ecclesiastes is about to serve up wisdom that transcends pixels, emojis, and status updates.

As we transition from the Green Zone to Relationships in the Digital Age, let's remember that our virtual interactions have real-world impacts. From the way we communicate to the friendships we cultivate, every like, comment, and share shapes the reputation of our social lives.

Chapter 6 is not just about navigating the complexities of online relationships but also about understanding the power we hold in shaping a positive and inclusive digital community. It's like being the architect of a virtual utopia, where kindness, respect, and genuine connections rule the digital landscape.

As we dive into the uncharted territories of Relationships in the Digital Age, let's keep the spirit of stewardship alive. Just as we've cared for our home in the Green Zone, now we embark on a journey to nurture the bonds that connect us in this vast digital universe.

Chapter 6 – Relationships in the Digital Age – is our chance to redefine what it means to be truly connected. Let's make it a chapter of compassion, understanding, and authentic relationships that withstand the tests of the online realm. Get ready to explore the digital heartbeat of connections, and may your digital adventures be filled with meaningful encounters.

As we open the virtual pages of Chapter 6, let the quest for genuine relationships in the digital age begin. Stay tuned, keep your emojis positive, and let's unravel the mysteries of human connections in the era of screens and pixels.

Chapter 6: Ecclesiastes 6 - Relationships in the Digital Age: Authenticity in a Virtual World

Welcome to Chapter 6 – where we're ditching the old-school relationship rulebook and diving headfirst into the digital deep end. Get ready for a wild ride through the binary jungles, the emoji oceans, and the meme-filled skies. Ecclesiastes is about to drop some wisdom on Relationships in the Digital Age.

Now, you might be thinking, "Wait, relationships in the digital age? Isn't that just a series of ones and zeros?" Well, buckle up, because we're about to decode the language of digital connections, swipe through the landscapes of virtual emotions, and navigate the social media maze like rockstars, or maybe not like rockstars. I guess it depends on which rockstars you follow.

Chapter 6 isn't your grandma's love letter; it's an emoji-filled, GIF-packed adventure through the realms of friendships, romances, and the mysterious world of online connections. It's like upgrading from a flip phone to the latest tech – but for your heart.

So, whether you're navigating the waters of online dating, deciphering cryptic DMs, or curating the perfect Instagram squad, Ecclesiastes has your back. It's time to rewrite the rules, remix the algorithms, and redefine what it means to be connected in this digital symphony of relationships.

Get ready to LOL, OMG, and maybe even shed a tear or two because Ecclesiastes is about to serve up a digital feast of wisdom. Whether you're swiping right, left, or just scrolling through the feeds of friendship, Chapter 6 is your backstage pass to the digital show of human connections.

As we embark on this quest into Relationships in the Digital Age, let's keep it real, keep it fun, and remember – in this chapter, emojis speak louder than words, and a well-timed GIF can say more than a thousand characters. Ready to decode the digital love language? Let the adventure begin!

Ecclesiastes 6 and the Virtual World

Ecclesiastes 6, provides intriguing insights into the pursuit of authenticity in a virtual world. Let's explore key verses that touch on themes related to genuine identity and the challenges posed by the digital realm:

6:9 - "Enjoy what you have rather than desiring what you don't have. Just dreaming about nice things is meaningless—like chasing the wind."

In a virtual world where curated images and idealized representations abound, this verse underscores the importance of finding contentment in the present moment. Pursuing an idealized online persona can be as elusive as chasing the wind, emphasizing the value of authenticity over virtual aspirations.

6:10 - "Everything has already been decided. It was known long ago what each person would be. So there's no use arguing with God about your destiny."

This verse challenges the notion of constant reinvention of self in the virtual space. While online platforms allow for self-expression, Ecclesiastes suggests recognizing the pre-determined nature of one's identity. Embracing authenticity involves acknowledging and being true to one's inherent nature.

6:11 - "The more words you speak, the less they mean. So what good are they?"

This verse highlights the potential emptiness of excessive self-expression in the virtual world flooded with text and messages. Authenticity is not measured by the quantity of words or posts but by the depth and sincerity of the message conveyed.

In summary, Ecclesiastes 6 encourages a thoughtful reflection on the pursuit of authenticity in the virtual world. It emphasizes finding contentment, embracing one's inherent identity, valuing meaningful communication over quantity, and acknowledging the potential challenges posed by systemic influences in the digital realm. Applying these insights, individuals can navigate the virtual world with a focus on authenticity and genuine self-expression.

Applying Wisdom to the Challenges of Building Authentic Relationships

In the digital era where virtual interactions often take center stage, the wisdom from Ecclesiastes 6 provides valuable insights on the challenges of building authentic relationships. Let's delve into how the verses from Ecclesiastes 6, using the New Living Translation (NLT), can be applied to the quest for genuine connections in a world dominated by the virtual realm:

Contentment in Virtual Spaces (Ecclesiastes 6:9, NLT):

In the virtual world, the constant desire for more followers, likes, or digital recognition can lead to a never-ending chase. Applying Ecclesiastes 6:9 encourages individuals to find contentment in their current online connections, fostering authenticity by valuing quality over quantity.

Authenticity in Digital Self-Presentation (Ecclesiastes 6:10, NLT):

Building authentic relationships online begins with accepting and presenting oneself genuinely. Ecclesiastes 6:10 encourages individuals to embrace their true identity rather than striving to be someone they are not. Authentic connections flourish when based on the honesty of digital self-presentation.

Quality over Quantity in Digital Communication (Ecclesiastes 6:11, NLT):

In the virtual world, where communication is abundant, Ecclesiastes 6:11 prompts reflection on the quality of digital interactions. Authentic relationships thrive on meaningful and intentional communication, emphasizing substance over sheer volume.

In essence, applying the wisdom from Ecclesiastes 6 to the challenges of building authentic relationships in a virtual world involves finding contentment, embracing one's true identity, prioritizing meaningful communication, fostering joy and acceptance in virtual connections, and navigating challenges with awareness. By incorporating these principles, individuals can navigate the digital landscape with authenticity and build genuine relationships amid virtual interactions.

Rediscovering Fulfillment in Genuine Connections

Let's talk about the ultimate quest: rediscovering fulfillment in the land of genuine connections. In a world where swipes, clicks, and likes often reign supreme, it's time to embark on a quest that's more epic than a meme going viral and more satisfying than finding the perfect GIF response.

1. The Uncharted Territory of Genuine LOLs:

Ever laughed so genuine it could power a small spaceship? Rediscovering fulfillment in genuine connections is like stumbling upon a treasure trove of unfiltered, belly-shaking laughter. So, ditch the virtual LOLs; let's aim for the kind that leaves you questioning your life choices – in a good way!

2. Emoji-Free Heart-to-Hearts:

In a world full of emojis, stickers, and digital hieroglyphics, rediscovering fulfillment means having heart-to-hearts that are emoji-free zones. It's like stripping away the filters and laying bare the raw, unfiltered emotions. Who needs a heart emoji when you can have the real deal?

3. Quality Over Quantity Messages:

Forget the endless stream of messages that flood your inbox like a digital tsunami. Rediscovering fulfillment is about quality over quantity. It's like savoring a gourmet meal instead of devouring a never-ending buffet. So, let's trade the message bombardment for messages that truly matter – the kind that makes your heart do a little happy dance.

4. GIFs Can't Replace Real Hugs:

As fun as GIFs are, they can't replace the warmth of a real hug. Rediscovering fulfillment means trading virtual embraces for the kind that you can feel in your bones. It's like upgrading from a pixelated hug to an HD, 3D, surround-sound embrace that leaves you feeling all fuzzy inside.

5. The Art of Meaningful Hangouts:

Hanging out in the virtual realm is cool, but rediscovering fulfillment involves mastering the art of meaningful hangouts. It's like turning a digital gathering into a symphony of shared experiences, where the pixels fade, and the real connections shine. So, let's plan hangouts that make memories, not just data usage.

6. Unfiltered Selfies – Imperfections Welcome:

Say goodbye to perfect angles and flawless filters. Rediscovering fulfillment is about embracing unfiltered selfies – imperfections and all. It's like saying, "Hey world, this is me, and I'm rocking it!" Because let's face it, perfection is overrated, and authenticity is the real MVP.

7. Digital Detox:

Sometimes, the road to rediscovering fulfillment involves a digital detox. It's like taking a break from the constant notifications and status updates to reconnect with the real world. Your mental health will thank you, and genuine connections will bloom like wildflowers in the spring.

So, fellow Connection Rediscoverers, let's embark on this epic journey to rediscover fulfillment in genuine connections. It's time to swipe right on authenticity, upgrade our virtual hangouts to unforgettable experiences, and embrace the joy that comes from real, unfiltered, and unabashedly genuine connections.

Discussion Questions

Discussion questions for Chapter 6 – Relationships in the Digital Age, along with activities to enhance engagement and reflection:

Authenticity Online:

How do you define authenticity in the digital realm? Can online connections truly reflect authentic relationships, or are they limited by the virtual medium?

Challenges in Virtual Relationships:

What are some challenges you've faced or observed in building genuine connections online? How do these challenges differ from face-to-face interactions?

Digital Persona vs. Real Self:
Do you feel there's a difference between your digital persona and your real self? How do you navigate presenting your authentic self in the digital world?

Impact of Social Media on Relationships:
How has social media influenced your relationships, both positively and negatively? Do you think it enhances or hinders the authenticity of connections?

Building Trust Online:
Trust is a crucial element in any relationship. How do you build and maintain trust in virtual relationships? Can online connections be as trustworthy as those formed offline?

Activities
Digital Detox Challenge:
Encourage participants to embark on a digital detox for a specified period (e.g., a day or a weekend). Reflect on how this break impacted their digital relationships and share insights during the next discussion.

Authenticity Audit:
Have participants conduct an "authenticity audit" of their online profiles. Ask them to assess whether their digital presence truly reflects their authentic selves. Share observations and discuss any adjustments they'd like to make.

Online Connection Reflection Journal:

Start an online connection reflection journal. Participants can document their thoughts and feelings about their online interactions, exploring what makes certain connections feel more authentic than others.

Virtual Storytelling Night:

Host a virtual storytelling night where participants share anecdotes about their most memorable online interactions. Encourage them to focus on moments that feel genuinely meaningful or authentic.

Create a Digital Code of Conduct:

Collaboratively create a digital code of conduct for your group or community. Discuss what values and behaviors should define your online interactions to foster a more authentic and positive digital space.

Remember, the goal is to facilitate open and honest conversations about digital relationships while engaging in activities that encourage participants to reflect on their own experiences and behaviors. Feel free to adapt these questions and activities to suit the dynamics of your group!

Conclusion

We've just wrapped up Chapter 6 – the epic saga of Relationships in the Digital Age. We've decoded emojis, navigated the maze of online connections, and maybe even found a virtual soulmate or two. But guess what? Our journey doesn't stop here; Chapter 7 is lurking around the corner, and it's all about facing uncertainty.

So, as we bid adieu to the virtual hugs, heart reactions, and the occasional online drama, get ready to embrace the next adventure. Chapter 7 isn't just about-facing uncertainty; it's a crash course in improv, where life's script takes unexpected twists, turns, and maybe a few plot twists worthy of a blockbuster.

So, fellow Uncertainty Conquerors, as we wave goodbye to the digital drama of Chapter 6, get ready to face the unknown with a wink, a smile, and maybe the hope of a time machine. Chapter 7 awaits, and it's not just a chapter; it's a choose-your-own-adventure book. Buckle up and let the ride continue!

Chapter 7: Ecclesiastes 7 - Facing Uncertainty: Navigating the Unknown in the 21st Century

Greetings, Bold Adventurers! Welcome to Chapter 7, an enthralling odyssey where uncertainty becomes the canvas for your unique saga. Visualize this chapter as an interactive, choose-your-own-adventure narrative, where every twist of the plot and every decision propels you further into uncharted territories.

In this realm of uncertainty, you're not just a reader; you're the protagonist of your story. What quest will you undertake as you navigate the twists and turns of life's unpredictable novel? Will you embark on a daring journey of self-discovery, chart the maze of life's decisions, or forge alliances with fellow travelers on this adventure of a lifetime?

Anticipate plot twists that rival the most suspenseful novels, keeping you on the edge of your seat. Chapter 7 is a page-turner, filled with surprises that challenge your resilience and reveal the beauty within life's unpredictable narrative.

Imagine life's uncertainties as a crossroads, where each choice leads to a different adventure. Will you take the road less traveled, dance through the wilderness, or build a rocket to explore uncharted territories? The possibilities are as limitless as the horizon.

Consider this chapter your toolkit for the unknown. Armed with wisdom, wit, and a dash of humor, you'll navigate uncertainty like a seasoned adventurer. It's time to wield your compass, don your adventurer's hat, and face the unknown with unwavering confidence.

Fear not, intrepid explorers, for you're not alone on this journey. Chapter 7 invites you to join a community of fellow adventurers, sharing tales of triumphs, challenges, and perhaps a few unexpected mishaps. Together, we'll discover the beauty in the uncertainty of life.

So, open the pages of Chapter 7, unfurl your map, and prepare to embark on a choose-your-own-adventure quest. Whether you choose the path of daring exploration or opt for the scenic route of introspection, remember: that uncertainty is not an obstacle but a thrilling invitation to craft your narrative. The adventure begins now!

Ecclesiastes 7 and the Unpredictability of Life

Ecclesiastes 7, through the lens of the New Living Translation (NLT), provides a profound perspective on the unpredictability of life. Let's delve into the wisdom encapsulated in this chapter:

7:13-14 - "Accept the way God does things, for who can straighten what he has made crooked? Enjoy prosperity while you can, but when hard times strike, realize that both come from God. Remember that nothing is certain in this life."

This passage underscores the fundamental truth that life's twists and turns are inherently unpredictable. The call to "accept the way God does things" serves as a reminder that the Godly order, as determined by a higher power, often operates in ways beyond our comprehension. Life's inherent crookedness is a testament to the complexity and unpredictability embedded in the fabric of existence.

The juxtaposition of prosperity and hardship is a key theme. The verse encourages us to embrace moments of prosperity while remaining cognizant that life's journey is a mosaic of both joy and challenge. The acknowledgment that both prosperity and adversity emanate from the divine source challenges us to seek meaning in every circumstance.

7:15 - "I have seen everything in this meaningless life, including the death of good young people and the long life of wicked people."

This verse unveils the seeming injustice and unpredictability of life. The observation that good young people may meet untimely deaths while the wicked may live long lives confronts our human understanding of fairness. Ecclesiastes 7 prompts contemplation on the mystery of life's outcomes and the realization that a just and predictable existence might be an elusive pursuit.

7:16-18 - "Don't be too virtuous, and don't be too wise. Why destroy yourself? Don't be too wicked or too foolish. Why die before your time? It is good to grasp the one and not let the other slip from your hand. For the one who fears God will avoid both extremes."

This passage advocates for a balanced approach to life, steering clear of extremes. The caution against excessive virtue or wisdom, as well as the warning against wickedness or foolishness, underscores the importance of navigating the unpredictable nature of life with prudence. The call to "fear God" emphasizes the wisdom of embracing a middle path, and avoiding the pitfalls of extremes.

In essence, Ecclesiastes 7 invites us to confront the inherent unpredictability of life. It encourages a nuanced understanding that embraces both prosperity and adversity as integral parts of our journey. The acknowledgment of life's uncertainties prompts reflection on our response to the unpredictable, urging us to seek wisdom and balance in navigating the intricacies of existence.

Finding Peace in an Uncertain World

In the wisdom literature of Ecclesiastes 7, there is a timeless and resonant message that speaks directly to the challenges of our modern world – the pursuit of peace amidst the pervasive anxiety and uncertainty that often defines our daily lives. Let's glean insights from Ecclesiastes 7, seeking wisdom to navigate the tumultuous waters of our contemporary existence.

Ecclesiastes 7:14 provides a grounding perspective in the face of anxiety stemming from the unpredictability of life. It encourages us not only to embrace moments of prosperity but also to recognize that hardship is an inevitable part of the human experience. Understanding that both joy and adversity emanate from a higher source invites us to cultivate a sense of resilience and acceptance in the face of life's uncertainties.

In the pursuit of peace, Ecclesiastes 7:16-18 advises against extremes. The modern world often pushes us towards excess – whether in the relentless pursuit of success or the overwhelming pressure of keeping up with a fast-paced digital society. This wisdom suggests finding a balanced approach, acknowledging that neither excessive virtue nor foolishness contributes to lasting peace. Instead, a balanced perspective, grounded in a reverence for the divine, can help navigate the complexities of the modern world.

Practical Insights for Finding Peace:

Cultivate Mindfulness:

Ecclesiastes 7 encourages an awareness of the present moment. In a world filled with constant stimuli, practicing mindfulness helps us find peace by anchoring us in the now and reducing anxiety about an uncertain future.

Embrace Resilience:

Acknowledging that both joy and adversity are part of life's journey fosters resilience. Embracing challenges as opportunities for growth can contribute to a sense of peace amid life's uncertainties.

Avoiding Extreme Expectations:

The advice against extremes suggests moderation in our expectations. Seeking balance in personal and professional pursuits, and avoiding the extremes of perfectionism or negligence, contributes to a more tranquil state of mind.

Foster a Spiritual Connection:

For those who find solace in spirituality, nurturing a connection with a higher power can be a source of peace. Recognizing that life's uncertainties are part of a larger plan can provide comfort in times of anxiety.

In Ecclesiastes 7, we find threads of timeless wisdom that, when woven into the fabric of our modern lives, offer guidance on finding peace amid the anxieties and uncertainties of today's world. It beckons us to navigate the complexities with balance, resilience, and a spiritual perspective, fostering a sense of tranquility even in life's unpredictability.

Embracing the Beauty of Life's Uncertainties

Life is the ultimate "Choose Your Own Adventure" book, where every twist, turn, and unexpected detour adds excitement to the narrative. Ecclesiastes 7 isn't just a chapter; it's your personalized quest in this interactive novel of existence.

Embrace the Unpredictable Plot: In the thrilling narrative of life, uncertainties are not plot holes; they are the surprise chapters that add spice to your adventure. Ecclesiastes 7 invites you to don your adventurer's hat, pick the path less travelled, and revel in the unexpected plot twists that make your story uniquely yours.

Navigate the Maze with a Wink and a Smile: Life's uncertainties are like a grand maze in your adventure book. Instead of getting lost in the labyrinth, imagine yourself navigating with a wink and a smile. Ecclesiastes suggests that approaching the twists and turns with a lighthearted spirit turns the maze into your playground.

Celebrate the Adventure Dance: Life's uncertainties aren't hurdles; they are dance partners in the grand adventure. Cue up your favorite soundtrack, take the lead, and dance through the twists and turns with style. Ecclesiastes encourages you to turn uncertainty into a dance, making every step part of your chosen adventure.

Pack Your Sense of Humor: Just like any great adventure, life is better with a sense of humor. Pack your wit, and when the storyline takes an unexpected turn, throw in a clever one-liner. Ecclesiastes 7 suggests that laughter is your secret weapon in navigating the unforeseen plot twists.

Forge Alliances with Uncertainty: Uncertainty is not the antagonist; it's your adventure ally. Ecclesiastes extends an invitation to make uncertainty part of your chosen adventure party. Together, you'll explore uncharted territories and uncover hidden gems in the pages of your life's novel.

So, intrepid explorers, as you open the pages of Ecclesiastes 7, see it not as a chapter but as a decision point in your "Choose Your Own Adventure" saga. Embrace the beauty of uncertainty, make bold choices, and revel in the joy of crafting your unique narrative. Your adventure awaits!

Discussion Questions

Embracing the Rollercoaster:

How do you personally approach life's uncertainties? Are you more inclined to resist, endure, or embrace the unpredictable twists and turns?

Balancing Act:

Ecclesiastes 7 advises against extremes. In what areas of your life do you find it challenging to strike a balance, and how might you navigate those situations more wisely?

Theme Park Mentality:

If life were a theme park, which ride or attraction would symbolize your approach to uncertainties? Share your choice and explain how it mirrors your perspective on life.

Uncertainty and Resilience:

How can acknowledging the unpredictability of life contribute to building resilience? Share examples from your own experiences or those of others.

The Role of Humor:

Ecclesiastes suggests packing a sense of humor for life's journey. How has humor helped you navigate uncertainties, and in what ways can it be a valuable tool in facing challenges?

Navigating the Maze:

Life's uncertainties are compared to a maze. How do you approach navigating through life's twists and turns? What strategies or mindsets help you find your way through challenges?

Choosing Your Adventure:
If life were a "Choose Your Own Adventure" book, what decisions or choices in your past do you think have significantly shaped your current narrative?

Dancing Through Challenges:
How can the concept of dancing through life's challenges be applied practically? Share personal anecdotes or examples of times when you turned adversity into a dance.

Facing Uncertainty with a Wink and a Smile:
Ecclesiastes encourages facing uncertainties with a wink and a smile. How might adopting a lighthearted approach positively impact your outlook on life's challenges?

Alliances with Uncertainty:
How can you shift your perspective to view uncertainty as an ally rather than an adversary in your life's adventure? Share strategies for forging alliances with the uncertainties you encounter.

These discussion questions are designed to spark thoughtful conversations about the insights from Ecclesiastes 7 and how they resonate with personal experiences and perspectives on navigating life's uncertainties.

Conclusion
Bravo, daring adventurers! You've just conquered the choose-your-own-adventure of Chapter 7, where life's uncertainties became the thrilling twists in your tale. But hold on tight; we're not closing the book just yet. Instead, we're stepping into Chapter 8—a treasure hunt for wisdom in a world that's like a puzzle with a gazillion pieces.

So, imagine Chapter 7 as the crazy adventure, and Chapter 8? Well, it's like putting on your explorer hat and grabbing a treasure map. Ecclesiastes is inviting us on a quest—a quest for wisdom.

Wisdom here isn't some dusty old bookish thing; it's more like the coolest tool in your adventure backpack. It helps you figure out the tricky parts of life, like finding your way through a jungle of tough decisions and information overload.

In the upcoming chapter, Ecclesiastes becomes your trusty handbook for making wise choices in our modern, sometimes confusing, world. Think of it as upgrading your decision-making skills so you can navigate the complexities of life like a pro.

And here's the kicker—wisdom isn't about being all serious and stern. Nope! It's about balancing the wild and the wise, like doing a skateboard trick on the edge of a cliff. Ecclesiastes is like your cool older friend who knows the ropes and is ready to spill the secrets on how to pull off the ultimate life stunts.

So, fellow adventurers, get ready for Chapter 8! It's not just the next chapter; it's a continuation of the epic adventure that is your life. Fasten your seatbelts, keep your eyes peeled for wisdom nuggets, and let's rock this next part of the quest together. Onwards to the treasure hunt!

Chapter 8: Ecclesiastes 8 - The Quest for Wisdom in a Complex World

Ahoy, fearless treasure hunters! As we swing into Chapter 8 of our grand adventure – Ecclesiastes, the vibe is shifting from choose-your-own-adventure books to Indiana Jones-style escapades. Picture yourself donning a fedora, cracking the whip, and stepping into the mystical world of wisdom. This is no ordinary chapter; it's a treasure hunt in the complex maze of existence.

In this installment, Ecclesiastes becomes your ancient map, guiding you through the intricate jungle of life's challenges. The quest? Oh, it's nothing short of an Indiana Jones blockbuster – a daring pursuit of the hidden gems of wisdom.

The scene is set. You, the intrepid explorer, are about to decipher the cryptic inscriptions on the Wisdom Map. Ecclesiastes 8 is your ticket to an adventure where each step reveals secrets to navigate the twists, turns, and booby traps of our modern, puzzling world.

Imagine the echoes of adventure as you delve into this chapter – your fedora tilted, torch flickering, and the quest for wisdom echoing through ancient corridors. Watch out for snakes! Ecclesiastes becomes your wise mentor, sharing the secrets that make decisions clearer, complexity conquerable, and life's puzzles solvable.

So, fellow treasure seekers, buckle up your metaphorical seatbelts, because Chapter 8 isn't just a chapter – it's an expedition. Grab your hat, ready your whip, and let's embark on an Indiana Jones-style quest for wisdom. Uncover the treasures, dodge the pitfalls, and let the adventure begin!

Exploring Ecclesiastes 8 in the Face of Complexity

In the heart of Ecclesiastes 8, we find ourselves on a thrilling quest for wisdom, armed with the ancient map of insights that guides us through the labyrinth of life's complexities. Ecclesiastes, our wise mentor, beckons us to embrace the challenges of a world where the puzzles are intricate, the decisions are nuanced, and the stakes are high.

8:1 - "How wonderful to be wise, to analyze and interpret things. Wisdom lights up a person's face, softening its harshness."

As we dive into this wisdom-laden chapter, Ecclesiastes sets the stage by painting a vivid picture of the beauty and power of wisdom. It's not just about accumulating knowledge; it's the art of analyzing, interpreting, and bringing light to the complexity that often shrouds our path. Wisdom, it seems, is the beacon that softens the harsh edges of our understanding.

8:5-6 "Those who obey him will not be punished. Those who are wise will find a time and a way to do what is right, for there is a time and a way for everything, even when a person is in trouble."

Here, Ecclesiastes whispers to us about the harmony between wisdom and righteous action. Wisdom isn't a mere intellectual exercise; it's the compass that guides us to navigate the complexities of life ethically and effectively. Even in times of trouble, the wise find a way to steer through the storms.

8:16-17 "In my search for wisdom and in my observation of people's burdens here on earth, I discovered that there is ceaseless activity, day and night. I realized

that no one can discover everything God is doing under the sun. Not even the wisest people discover everything, no matter what they claim."

Ecclesiastes, the sage explorer, acknowledges the ceaseless activity of life and the vastness of what lies beneath the sun. Even the wisest among us, in their quest for understanding, cannot unravel the entirety of God's intricate design. It's a humbling realization that wisdom, though a powerful guide, doesn't grant us omniscience.

In the treasure trove of Ecclesiastes 8, we uncover not just principles but a living guide for the quest of wisdom in our intricate world. It's an invitation to wield wisdom as a lantern, illuminating the dark corners of complexity, and navigating the mysterious landscape of our existence with courage and discernment.

Navigating the Intricacies of the 21st-century World

In the bustling landscape of the 21st century, Ecclesiastes 8 unfolds as a timeless compass, offering insights that resonate with the intricacies of our modern world. As we venture into applying its teachings, let's harness the wisdom of Ecclesiastes to navigate the complexities that define our era.

Wisdom Illuminates Digital Dilemmas: In a world immersed in technology and digital dilemmas, Ecclesiastes 8 encourages us to seek wisdom as a guiding light. It's not just about analyzing data but interpreting the implications, and making informed choices in a realm where information overload can cloud judgment.

Time and Ethical Decision-Making: In an age where decisions are often made in haste, Ecclesiastes 8 whispers about the significance of time and ethical decision-making. Wisdom calls us to pause, reflect, and find the right time and manner to address the multifaceted challenges posed by rapidly evolving technologies and societal shifts.

Acknowledging Limits in the Information Age: Amidst the ceaseless activity of the information age, Ecclesiastes humbles us by reminding us that even the wisest cannot fathom everything. It's an invitation to acknowledge the limits of our understanding, fostering humility in an era where the pursuit of knowledge often feels boundless.

Wisdom in the Social Media Arena: In the realm of social media, where voices clamor for attention, Ecclesiastes guides us to find the balance between being informed and avoiding the pitfalls of misinformation. Wisdom becomes the filter through which we engage, discern, and contribute meaningfully in the ever-expanding digital conversation.

Applying Wisdom to Global Challenges: Ecclesiastes 8 extends its wisdom to global challenges, urging us to navigate issues like climate change, social inequality, and geopolitical tensions with discernment. Wisdom encourages responsible stewardship of the planet and a commitment to justice and equity.

Balancing Digital Connectivity and Authentic Connections: In a world of hyper-connectivity, Ecclesiastes teaches us to balance the digital with the authentic. Wisdom prompts us to craft genuine connections amid the virtual noise, emphasizing the quality of relationships over the quantity of online interactions.

As we apply the teachings of Ecclesiastes 8 to our 21st-century journey, let wisdom be our guide through the labyrinth of technological advancements, societal complexities, and global challenges. It's an invitation to infuse our digital existence with timeless insights, fostering a harmonious coexistence with the intricacies of our ever-evolving world.

Seeking Timeless Wisdom in a Fast-paced Society

Picture this: you, decked out in your Indiana Jones gear, hat tilted just right, whip cracking in the air. Now, why this dramatic setup? Because in the warp-speed society we find ourselves in, seeking timeless wisdom is like embarking on an epic quest for the Holy Grail. Welcome to the Indiana Jones of the mind, my friends – where wisdom is the treasure, we're after!

Navigating the Fast-Paced Jungle: In a world moving faster than Indy escaping a boulder, Ecclesiastes 8 becomes our trusty map. It's the ancient GPS guiding us through the bustling jungle of information overload, helping us dodge the quicksand of superficial knowledge.

Wisdom: Your Fedora in the Storm: Imagine wisdom as your trusty fedora – shielding you from the torrential downpour of fleeting trends and instant gratification. Ecclesiastes invites us to equip ourselves with this timeless accessory as we weather the storms of a society racing faster than a speeding ticket.

Deciphering the Modern-Day Riddles: Our quest involves deciphering modern-day riddles – the enigma of social media, the conundrums of ethical tech use, and the labyrinth of global challenges. Ecclesiastes, our ancient sage, whispers clues on how to unlock these mysteries with wisdom as our key.

The Wisdom Whip Cracks: Just as Indy's whip cracks in the face of danger, wisdom is our dynamic tool against the perils of a frantic lifestyle. It's the whip that snaps us back to reality, urging us to pause, reflect, and make intentional choices in the whirlwind.

Wisdom's Ark of Balance: Ecclesiastes 8 is our Ark of the Covenant, safeguarding the balance between the demands of the modern world and the pursuit of timeless truths. It's not about slowing down the chase but ensuring our quest is filled with purpose and meaning.

The Temple of Genuine Connections: As we venture into the Temple of Social Media, Ecclesiastes shows us how to navigate the traps and pitfalls. Wisdom becomes our guide, helping us build genuine connections in a virtual world saturated with fleeting trends and viral noise.

So, intrepid seekers of timeless wisdom, as you continue on this Indiana Jones-style adventure through Ecclesiastes 8, remember: you're not just racing against time; you're on a quest for wisdom that transcends the ages. Fasten your fedora, and crack that whip of discernment!

Discussion Questions

Wisdom in Fast-Paced Times:

How do you interpret the concept of seeking wisdom in a fast-paced society as presented in Ecclesiastes 8?

In what ways can wisdom be a valuable asset in navigating the challenges of a high-speed lifestyle?

The Time and Ethics Equation:

Ecclesiastes 8 talks about finding the right time for everything and ethical decision-making. How can this wisdom be applied to time management and decision-making in our modern lives?

Digital Dilemmas and Wisdom:
In the era of information overload and digital dilemmas, how can wisdom serve as a guide for responsible engagement with technology and online content?

Acknowledging Limits in the Information Age:
Ecclesiastes acknowledges the limits of human understanding. How can recognizing these limits impact our approach to acquiring knowledge and information in the information age?

Applying Wisdom Globally:
Ecclesiastes 8 encourages applying wisdom to global challenges. How can individual actions, guided by wisdom, contribute to addressing broader societal and global issues?

Activities
Wisdom Journal:
Create a wisdom journal where you record insights from Ecclesiastes 8 and reflect on how they can be applied to various aspects of your life, especially in the context of the fast-paced society we live in.

Digital Detox Challenge:
Take a weekend digital detox challenge. Disconnect from social media and technology, and afterward, discuss how this experience aligns with the wisdom discussed in Ecclesiastes 8.

Ethical Decision-Making Scenario:
Craft a scenario reflecting a real-life ethical dilemma, and discuss how applying the wisdom from Ecclesiastes 8 might influence decision-making in that situation.

Wisdom in Action Project:
Initiate a community project or personal initiative guided by the principles of wisdom discussed in Ecclesiastes 8. Share your experiences and reflections with a discussion group.

Global Wisdom Roundtable:
Organize a roundtable discussion on applying wisdom to global challenges. Explore how collective wisdom and informed decision-making can contribute to addressing issues such as climate change, social justice, and global cooperation.

Technology and Mindfulness Workshop:
Conduct a workshop on mindful technology use, discussing practical tips for staying connected without being overwhelmed. Share strategies on how wisdom can be applied to foster a healthy relationship with digital tools.

These discussion questions and activities are designed to encourage thoughtful reflection on the insights from Ecclesiastes 8 and provide practical avenues for applying wisdom in the context of our fast-paced, technologically-driven society.

Conclusion

With the dust settling on our fedoras and our wisdom whips coiled, Chapter 8 in our Indiana Jones-style escapade through Ecclesiastes concludes. We've plunged into the fast-paced jungles, decrypted the ancient map of wisdom, and emerged not only wiser but ready for what's next.

But fear not, for our adventure is far from its final act! Chapter 9 beckons, where "The Equality of Time and Chance" takes center stage. Picture it as stepping into a mystical chamber, where time and chance engage. Ecclesiastes serves as our enigmatic guide.

Envision Chapter 9 as a sprawling desert, where time shifts like sand beneath our feet. Ecclesiastes invites us to traverse this desert, recognizing time as the great equalizer – an ancient concept as enduring as the pyramids.

However, we need to hold onto your hats, fellow adventurers! Chance becomes the wild card, the unpredictable element that can sway the game in unforeseen ways. Ecclesiastes encourages us to grasp the interplay between time and chance, where the unexpected often steals the spotlight.

As we press forward, wisdom becomes our guide, leading us through the twisted landscape of time and chance. Ecclesiastes murmurs secrets on how to navigate this desert, embracing both the foreseeable and the unforeseen with grace.

Chapter 9 isn't merely a continuation; it's a gateway to unraveling the enigmas of existence. Picture it as a concealed chamber, found under the sands of the desert, filled with ancient scrolls that unveil the secrets of how time and chance weave their tales in life's grand adventure.

So, intrepid seekers of wisdom, tighten your fedoras, crack your whips, and brace yourselves for another enthralling chapter in our saga. Chapter 9 guarantees not just equality but a revelation of where time and chance hold the keys to the next thrilling adventure.

As we bid adieu to Chapter 8, remember: it's not the culmination of the quest but a bridge to the next treasure trove of timeless insights. Onwards, fellow adventurers, to the uncharted territories of Chapter 9!

Chapter 9: Ecclesiastes 9 - The Equality of Time and Chance: Embracing Life's Opportunities

Buckle up for the next stretch of our adventure through Ecclesiastes. Chapter 9 is about to unfold, and it's like stumbling upon a secret vault of ancient revelations. Get ready for "The Equality of Time and Chance" where our time machine awaits to show you all of life's opportunities for us to embrace!

Picture this chapter as a vast desert – time, the ever-shifting sands beneath our snazzy boots, and chance, the wild gusts of unpredictability shaping our journey. Ecclesiastes invites us to waltz into the wild west of time and chance, encouraging us to embrace life's opportunities like a cowboy finding the perfect horse to ride.

So, sandal up, adventurers! Chapter 9 is our invitation to ride into the sunset that governs our existence. Let's unravel the secrets of seizing life's opportunities, understanding that in the Wild West, every moment is a little bit unknown.

As we meander through this desert of possibilities, let Ecclesiastes be our funky guide, showing us how to recognize, snatch, and revel in the opportunities popping up in our journey. Onwards, fearless explorers, to a chapter bursting with equality, opportunities, and a vibrant life!

Reflecting on Ecclesiastes 9

Let's mosey on down to Ecclesiastes 9 in the Good Book, pardner, and take a closer look at some verses from the New Living Translation (NLT). This here's a wild west roundup of wisdom, so hitch up your spurs and let's wrangle some reflections from the cosmic corral.

9:7 - So go ahead. Eat your food with joy, and drink your wine with a happy heart, for God approves of this!

There's a call to appreciate the moments we're given on this Wild West trail. Each day, each opportunity is a gift, and it encourages us to tip our hats to the high noon sun in gratitude.+

9:10 - Whatever you do, do well. For when you go to the grave, there will be no work or planning or knowledge or wisdom.

Verse 10 calls for a proactive stance – to seize the day, or in cowboy lingo, rope in their opportunities. It's a call to action, a nudge to make the most of the Wild West rodeo while the sun's still setting on the horizon.

9:11 - I have observed something else under the sun. The fastest runner doesn't always win the race, and the strongest warrior doe not always win the battle. The wise sometimes go hungry, and the skillful are not necessarily wealthy. And those who are educated don't always lead successful lives. It is all decided by chance, by being in the right place at the right time.

Verse 11 in Ecclesiastes 9 talks about time and chance happening to them all, much like the winds that sweep across a prairie. It's a reminder that, in this cosmic rodeo, everyone, no matter their brand or badge, faces the same ol' sunlit horizon.

9:12 - People can never predict when hard times might come. Like fish in a net or birds in a trap, people are caught by sudden tragedy.

Verse 12 introduces chance as a wild card, stirring up the dust in the saloon. Life's opportunities, it says, often emerge unpredictably like a maverick causing a ruckus in the ol' town. It's a reminder that, in this rodeo, unpredictability is the name of the game.

Encouraging a Mindset of Embracing Opportunities

Gather 'round as we rustle up some wisdom from the Wild West pages of Ecclesiastes 9. It's time for a heart-to-heart, a little campfire chat under the prairie stars, about embracing opportunities with a cowboy spirit.

Now, Ecclesiastes 9 talks about time and chance happening to us all, much like the winds that sweep across the prairie. So, let me share a piece of sage advice from these trails: when life throws a lasso your way, don't just watch it swing by; give it a hearty yank and hop on that opportunity like it's the wildest bronco in the corral.

In the good book, it says, "Whatever your hand finds to do, do it with all your might." That's the cowboy way, ain't it? When you see a chance, rope it, ride it, and give it everything you got. Life's a rodeo, and you're the star of the show.

Now, reckon this: life, much like a tumbleweed rolling through the plains, is unpredictable. Opportunities come and go like gusts of wind, but that's what makes the ride worthwhile. Don't be sittin' on the fence, wondering if you should grab that lasso. Seize it! Rope it! Ride it out like the true cowboy or cowgirl you are.

There's a call in these verses to appreciate the moments, to tip your hat to the high noon sun. Every day is a gift, and every opportunity is a chance to dance in the moonlight of this rodeo. So, let gratitude be your sidekick as you rustle up those opportunities.

Remember, on this Wild West journey of life, you're not alone. We're all riders on this trail, facing the same sunlit horizon. So, saddle up, partner. Take the reins of those opportunities and ride 'em like you're chasing the sunset.

In the spirit of Ecclesiastes 9, let's be cowboys and cowgirls who embrace the unpredictability, seize the chances, and dance with gratitude under the vast prairie sky. The corral is open, and the opportunities are waiting to be roped. So, go on and ride, ride like there's no tomorrow!

Cultivating Resilience in the Face of Life's Uncertainties

Life on this wild west frontier can be as unpredictable as a tumbleweed in the prairie wind but fear not. It's time to saddle up and wrangle some wisdom on cultivating resilience in the face of life's uncertainties.

In the rodeo of existence, uncertainties are like wild broncos – you never quite know how they'll buck and kick. But here's the thing, partner, resilience is your trusty lasso. It's the skill of not just staying in the saddle but bouncing back with a whoop and a holler every time life tries to throw you off.

Ecclesiastes 9, that guidebook, whispers about the unpredictability of time and chance. Much like the winds that sweep across the prairie, life's twists and turns are bound to come. But cultivating resilience is like being a seasoned cowboy or cowgirl – you learn to ride the storms with grit and grace.

Now, resilience isn't about being stoic like a weathered desert rock. No sir, it's about bending like a willow in the wind, knowing when to yield and when to stand tall. It's about turning setbacks into setups for a grand comeback.

Here are a few trail-worthy tips for cultivating resilience:

Ride the Storms, Don't Dodge Them: Life isn't all sunshine and cacti. Embrace the storms, knowing that every downpour makes the prairie bloom. Resilience is about facing challenges head-on, like a cowboy facing a stampede.

Flex Those Mental Muscles: Resilience is a mental workout, flexing those cognitive muscles. It's about adapting, adjusting, and rustling up a positive mindset even when the corral seems a tad unruly.

Lean on Your Posse: Just like a cowboy relies on their posse, lean on your friends, family, and mentors. In the rodeo, having a support network can make all the difference when you're navigating rough terrain.

Find the Silver Spurs: In every challenge, look for the silver spurs – those nuggets of wisdom, growth, and strength. Resilience is about turning setbacks into stepping stones on this Wild West trail.

Dance with Gratitude: Even when the prairie wind howls, tip your hat to the high noon sun. Cultivate gratitude for the moments of calm between the storms. It's the cowboy's way of finding peace amidst the chaos.

Remember, partner, cultivating resilience is not just about surviving; it's about thriving on this Wild West journey. So, saddle up, ride out those uncertainties, and let resilience be your guide in the grand rodeo.

Discussion Questions
Riding the Plains:
How does the concept of time treating everyone equally resonate with your own experiences in facing opportunities in life?

In what ways can acknowledging the equality of time and chance influence our perspectives on success and achievement?

Chance: The Whimsical Maverick:
How do you view the role of chance in life, especially considering the unpredictability mentioned in Verse 12?

Can you share a personal experience where an unexpected opportunity or challenge changed the course of your journey?

Seizing the Sunset:
Ecclesiastes 9:10 encourages proactive engagement with opportunities. How do you interpret the idea of doing whatever your hand finds to do with all your might?

What challenges or fears might prevent individuals from seizing opportunities, and how can one overcome them?

An Invitation to Gratitude at High Noon:
How can incorporating gratitude into our daily lives enhance our experience of opportunities, as suggested in Verse 7?

In what ways can expressing gratitude impact our overall well-being and resilience in the face of uncertainties?

Cultivating Resilience:
How can the principles discussed in Ecclesiastes 9 contribute to building resilience in individuals and communities?

Share personal strategies for cultivating resilience in the face of life's uncertainties, drawing from both the scripture and your own experiences.

Feel free to adapt these questions to fit the context of your discussion, and enjoy wrangling up some insightful reflections!

Conclusion

As our time-traveling machine whirs and hums, carrying us away from the wide-open plains of opportunities in the Wild West, we bid a temporary adieu to Ecclesiastes 9. But fret not, for our journey through time and space is far from over.

In this wild west rodeo of life, Ecclesiastes 9 has been our trusty guide, reminding us of the equality of time and chance, urging us to seize the sunset with all our might, and encouraging a dance of gratitude under the high noon sun. As we hang our hats on the hitching post of Chapter 9, we carry the wisdom of embracing life's uncertainties and cultivating resilience in our saddlebags.

Now, as our time-travelling contraption gears up for the next leap, we're about to embark on a thrilling escapade into Chapter 10. The landscape may shift, but the journey continues. So, tighten your space-time spurs and adjust your chronal chaps, for we're about to navigate the twists and turns of folly and wisdom in the vast Information Age.

Chapter 10 is like a GPS for the digital trails of today, guiding us through the labyrinth of information, decisions, and the dance between folly and wisdom. As we ride the digital currents, let's keep our wits sharp, our insights keen, and our compasses true.

So, fellow time-travelers, saddle up for the next leg of our expedition. Chapter 10 awaits, and who knows what pearls of wisdom and celestial revelations it holds for us in the ever-evolving saga.

As Ecclesiastes 9 fades into the horizon, let's tip our hats to the lessons learned, the opportunities seized, and the resilience cultivated. Onward we ride, into the Information Age, where the digital winds whisper tales of folly and wisdom, awaiting our eager exploration.

May your time-travelling adventures be filled with wonders, and may the pages of Chapter 10 unfold like a star-studded map guiding us through the constellations of knowledge and discernment. Until our time-travelling paths cross again, keep the campfire burning, and may the dust settle gently on your trail.

Chapter 10: Ecclesiastes 10 - Navigating Folly and Wisdom in the Information Age

As our time-travelling machine hurtles through the currents, it's time to unsheathe our digital lassos and prepare for a wild ride through Chapter 10 of Ecclesiastes. Our destination: the ever-shifting landscapes of the Information Age, where the dance between folly and wisdom takes center stage.

In this odyssey, Ecclesiastes 10 becomes our trusty star map, guiding us through the labyrinth of the Information Age – an era where the digital winds whisper, the data streams flow, and the currents of information swell like a river in the early days of Spring. As we embark on this journey, saddle up and don your virtual chaps, for we're about to navigate the uncharted territories where bits and bytes dance in the saloon.

Chapter 10 beckons us to become cartographers, steering our time-travelling vessel through the rapids of decisions, the vast plains of information overload, and the winding trails where folly and wisdom often cross paths in the digital wilderness. It's a frontier where the stakes are high, the algorithms are enigmatic, and discernment becomes our compass in the vast sea of data.

So, fellow adventurers, let's embrace the challenges and revelations of Ecclesiastes 10. As we delve into the code of navigating folly and wisdom in the Information Age, may our digital spurs be sharp, our data senses keen, and our wisdom profound.

Join me as we embark on this expedition, riding the binary waves, decoding the algorithms, and uncovering the timeless truths that resonate in the interconnected realms of technology and wisdom. Get ready to chart your course through the symphony of Ecclesiastes 10 – where the dance of folly and wisdom takes on a digital tempo.

Analyzing Ecclesiastes 10

10:1 - As dead flies cause even a bottle of perfume to stink, so a little foolishness spoils great wisdom and honor.

Ecclesiastes 10 starts by reminding us that folly is like dead flies that affect the bottle of perfume and how it smells. In the Information Age, a single click, a digital ripple, can send echoes across the vast expanse of the internet. Folly, much like a wild stallion, can run rampant if left unchecked, leading us down rabbit holes of misinformation and confusion.

10:2 - A wise person chooses the right road; a fool takes the wrong one.

On the flip side, Ecclesiastes 10 extols the virtues of wisdom, likening it to a wise person's face illuminating their way. In the wilderness of information, wisdom becomes our North Star, guiding us through the labyrinth of choices and aiding in deciphering the signals from the noise.

10:10 - Using a dull ax requires great strength, so sharpen the blade. That's the value of wisdom; it helps you succeed.

Ecclesiastes 10:10 paints a vivid picture of a dull ax requiring more strength and wisdom for effective chopping. In the digital forest, our tools are the algorithms, apps, and platforms we wield. Without wisdom, our digital axes may become dull, requiring more effort to cut through the dense thicket of information.

10:11 - If a snake bites before you charm it, what's the use of being a snake charmer?

Verse 11 warns that the words of a fool lead to quarrels, much like a snake lurking in the grass. In the online ecosystem, words hold immense power, capable of sparking debates or fostering understanding. Folly in communication can sow discord, while wisdom can cultivate harmony.

10:15 - Fools are so exhausted by a little work that they can't even find their way home.

Ecclesiastes 10:15 speaks of the toil of fools wearing them out because they don't know the way to town. In the Information Age, the digital landscape can be a sprawling city, and without wisdom, one can easily get lost in the labyrinth of algorithms and data.

In Ecclesiastes 10, the symphony of folly and wisdom resonates with the challenges and opportunities presented by the Information Age. As we ride the digital trails, may we sharpen our discernment, embrace wisdom as our guide, and navigate the vast highway of information with grace and insight.

Application & Reflection

As we hitch our digital steeds and prepare to explore the sage insights of Ecclesiastes 10, let's rustle up some wisdom to discern and navigate the vast sea of information in this digital age.

1. Sharpen Your Digital Lasso: Ecclesiastes 10 compares a dull ax to the need for more strength. In the digital frontier, your tools are your digital lassos – apps, algorithms, and platforms. Keep them sharp by staying informed, updating your skills, and understanding the ever-evolving landscape of the online world.

Reflection: How can you sharpen your digital tools to navigate the digital wilderness more effectively?

2. Watch for Serpents in the Grass: Ecclesiastes 10 warns of quarrels sparked by foolish words, akin to a snake in the grass. In the online realm, choose your words wisely. Be aware of the potential impact your words may have and strive for constructive communication rather than contributing to digital discord.

Reflection: How can you contribute to a more positive online discourse, and what strategies can you employ to avoid unnecessary quarrels?

3. Build Your Navigation Skills: Just as a fool wears themselves out without knowing the way to town, navigating the digital landscape without a sense of direction can be exhausting. Develop your digital navigation skills – understand how algorithms work, critically evaluate information, and be intentional about your online journey.

Reflection: What steps can you take to enhance your digital navigation skills and avoid the toil of getting lost in the vast sea of information?

4. Cultivate a Face of Wisdom: Ecclesiastes 10 compares the face of a wise person to a beacon of light. In the digital age, let wisdom illuminate your online presence. Be discerning about the content you create and share. Consider the potential impact of your digital footprint on others and the digital atmosphere at large.

Reflection: How can you cultivate a digital presence that reflects wisdom and contributes positively to the online community?

5. Collaborate in the Digital Town: Ecclesiastes 10:15 speaks of the fool toiling without knowing the way to town. In the digital town, collaboration is key. Connect with others, share insights, and learn from the collective wisdom of the online community. Together, we can navigate the digital wilderness more effectively.

Reflection: How can you actively engage in online communities to enhance your understanding and contribute to shared wisdom?

As we ride the digital trails of Ecclesiastes 10, may these insights guide us in discerning and navigating the vast sea of information in the Information Age. So, tighten those digital spurs, adjust your virtual hat, and let's chart a course through the data waves with wisdom and discernment.

Cultivating Discernment

In a world where information flows like a river, cultivating discernment is like donning a spacesuit to navigate the vast expanse of the digital cosmos. Let's wrangle some wisdom to ride the currents and master the art of distinguishing the Godly signal from the noise.

1. Mindfulness: In the whirlwind of digital data, practicing mindfulness is key. Pause, take a breath, and be present in the digital moment. Mindfulness allows you to engage with information more consciously, helping you sift through the clutter with a focused mind.

Reflection: How can you incorporate moments of mindfulness into your digital routine to enhance discernment?

2. Critical Constellation Analysis: Just as an astronomer studies constellations, becomes a critical analyst of the digital stars. Question the sources, cross-reference information, and peer through the telescope of skepticism. Scrutinize the patterns in the digital sky to discern the truth from the digital nebula.

Reflection: What strategies can you employ to critically analyze information sources in the digital universe?

3. Nebula of Nuanced Understanding: The digital cosmos is filled with nuances and shades of meaning. Cultivate a nebula of nuanced understanding by exploring different perspectives. Embrace the complexity of issues and resist the temptation of oversimplified cosmic narratives.

Reflection: How can you actively seek out diverse perspectives to enhance your discernment in the digital galaxy?

4. Quantum Information Verification: In a quantum age of information, verify the authenticity of data like a digital physicist. Check the reliability of sources, fact-check information, and be wary of hoaxes. Ensure that the information particles you encounter are grounded in the laws of truth.

Reflection: What steps can you take to verify the accuracy of information in your digital explorations?

5. Digital Detox: Even navigators need a break. Periodic digital detoxes are essential to recalibrate your discernment compass. Step away from the digital noise, immerse yourself in the analog universe, and return with a refreshed perspective.

Reflection: How can you integrate regular digital detoxes into your cosmic journey to maintain discernment clarity?

6. Celestial Community Consultation: Just as astronomers collaborate, consult your community. Engage in discussions, seek guidance from peers, and share your insights. The collective wisdom of the digital constellations can be a valuable resource in refining your discernment skills.

Reflection: How can you actively participate in digital communities to enhance your collective discernment?

As we navigate the sea of information, let discernment be your guiding star. With mindful exploration, critical analysis, nuanced understanding, rigorous verification, occasional detox, and collaboration, you'll ride the digital waves with confidence and discerning grace.

Discussion Questions

Let's lasso up some thought-provoking questions for a roundtable discussion on Ecclesiastes 10:

Digital Lassos and Sharpened Axes:

How do you keep your digital tools sharp in the Information Age, and what strategies can one employ to navigate the digital wilderness more effectively?

Words: Snakes or Songbirds?

In your experience, how have words, both online and offline, influenced discussions and relationships? Share examples of the impact of communication in the digital landscape.

The Toil of Navigation:

Ecclesiastes 10:15 compares a fool's toil to someone not knowing the way to town. How do you navigate the digital town, and how has wisdom played a role in avoiding the toil of online confusion?

Cultivating a Face of Wisdom:

Reflect on the concept of cultivating a face of wisdom in the digital realm. How can individuals contribute to a more positive online presence, and what impact can this have on the broader digital community?

The Serpent in the Digital Garden:

Ecclesiastes 10:11 warns about words leading to quarrels like a snake in the grass. Discuss instances where online communication led to disagreements and explore strategies for fostering constructive digital discourse.

Navigation Skills:

How do you develop and enhance your digital navigation skills? Share tips on staying informed, understanding algorithms, and critically evaluating information online.

Collaboration in the Digital Town:
Ecclesiastes 10:15 emphasizes the importance of collaboration in the digital town. How do you actively engage with online communities, and how has collective wisdom influenced your digital journey?

Online Discernment:
In a world flooded with information, how do you cultivate discernment? Share practices and strategies that help you distinguish between reliable and unreliable digital information.

Impact of Online Words:
Ecclesiastes 10:11 mentions that the words of a fool can lead to quarrels. Reflect on the impact of words in the digital landscape, both positive and negative. How can individuals contribute to a healthier online communication culture?

Balancing Digital and Analog:
How do you strike a balance between your digital and analog life? Share experiences of digital detoxes or moments where you consciously chose to engage with the analog world.

Feel free to round up your posse and rustle up some profound insights with these questions!

Conclusion

Adventurers of the digital age, as we bid farewell to the trails of Ecclesiastes 10, let's strap into our futuristic time machines, complete with flying cars and holographic guides. The Information Age has been our playground, and now, the horizon of Chapter 11 awaits us, promising a glimpse into the future of investments and dividends.

In this futuristic odyssey, Ecclesiastes 10 has been our trusty star map, guiding us through the digital constellations, warning of the pitfalls of folly, and equipping us with the discernment tools for navigating the sea of information. As we fasten our seatbelts for the quantum leap into Ecclesiastes 11, let's set our sights on investing in the future with flair.

Ecclesiastes 10 has prepared us to soar through the digital skies, avoiding the turbulence of folly and navigating with the precision of wisdom. As we transition to Chapter 11, imagine the digital wings of our time machines carrying us into a future where information flows like streams of stardust, ready for us to harness.

Chapter 11 beckons us to become investors in the grand symphony of the future. Picture ourselves not as mere spectators but as active participants, making strategic investments in the unfolding narrative of our digital destiny. What ventures shall we undertake, and how will our investments shape the future landscape?

Ecclesiastes 10 reminds us of the impact of our digital words, resonating like echoes in the vast canyon. In Chapter 11, let's consider the echoes we wish to send into the future. How can our investments in digital communication reverberate positively, leaving a legacy for generations to come?

Just as Ecclesiastes 10 nudged us to be stewards of digital resources, envision a future where our investments extend beyond personal gain. How can we practice futuristic stewardship, ensuring that our digital choices contribute to the sustainability and well-being of the community?

In Ecclesiastes 10, we learned the importance of navigating the digital wilderness with discernment. As we approach Chapter 11, consider the future as a complex algorithm of time, awaiting our navigation skills. How can we decipher the code of investments, making choices that resonate across the temporal tapestry of tomorrow?

As we lift off into the future with the propulsion of Ecclesiastes 11, may our investments be guided by the wisdom acquired in the classrooms of the past chapters. The digital highways of the future await our footprints, and our time-travelling journey continues with each turn of the celestial page. Onward to the investments and futuristic revelations that Chapter 11 holds for us!

Chapter 11: Ecclesiastes 11 - Investing in the Future: Balancing Risk and Reward

As we dust off the digital residue from our time machines and step into the future, Chapter 11 welcomes us to a high-tech arena of investments, where flying cars zip by and holographic billboards paint the skyline. Fasten your seatbelts, because we're diving headfirst into the realm of tomorrow: "Investing in the Future – Balancing Risk and Reward."

In this futuristic odyssey, we're not just stargazers; we're venture capitalists, equipped with hoverboards and algorithmic crystal balls. The future is our playground, and as we explore the possibilities of Ecclesiastes 11, let's do it with a touch of wit and a strategic eye for balancing the scales of risk and reward.

As we look around at the holographic cityscape of the future, investing is no longer confined to traditional markets. It's about strapping on our digital wings and soaring through the cloud-strewn realms of opportunity. Will we glide smoothly or perform daring loops in this high-flying investment adventure?

In this brave new world, quantum leaps in technology have transformed the investment landscape. No longer bound by the constraints of the past, we find ourselves on the precipice of futuristic investment strategies. What quantum leaps will we take to ensure our investments ride the wave of the future?

The future isn't a linear highway; it's a time-stream with bends and turns. Ecclesiastes 11 beckons us to be savvy navigators, balancing on the surfboard of risk while riding the waves of potential rewards. How will we ride the time stream, avoiding the rapids and catching the investment swells?

Say goodbye to traditional portfolios; in this future, holographic portfolios dance before us, showcasing the diversity of our investments. Ecclesiastes 11 encourages us to diversify, but in this brave new world, how will we embrace digital diversification to ride out the storms of uncertainty?

As we glide over the future's skyline on hoverboards, Ecclesiastes 11 prompts us to consider ethical investments and stewardship. How can we be responsible stewards of our investments, ensuring they contribute positively to the future landscape?

In the pages of Ecclesiastes 11, the future unfolds before us as a canvas of opportunity, with hoverboards, holograms, and high-stakes investments. So, fellow time-traveling investors, as we embark on this futuristic financial escapade, let's balance risk and reward with a dash of humor and a strategic eye for the dividends that lie ahead!

Delving into Ecclesiastes 11

A holographic guide to casting seeds into the vast time-stream of destiny. Let's navigate this landscape with the timeless wisdom of Ecclesiastes 11 as our compass.

11:1 -" Send your grain across the seas, and in time, profits will flow back to you."

In this digital age, sending your grain upon the waters may seem peculiar. Yet, Ecclesiastes invites us to sow our efforts generously, akin to launching digital ventures. The currents of time carry our efforts, and in the future, the harvest may emerge in unexpected waves of success.

11:4 - "Farmers who wait for perfect weather never plant. If they watch every cloud, they never harvest."

This verse challenges us to transcend hesitation and boldly sow seeds, even in uncertain times. In the future's digital fields, waiting for the perfect conditions may hinder progress. By navigating the gusts of change and uncertainty, we can embrace the potential for a rich harvest.

11:5 - "Just as you cannot understand the path of the wind or the mystery of a tiny baby growing in its mother's womb,[c] so you cannot understand the activity of God, who does all things."

Much like the mysteries of creation, unfolds in ways beyond our comprehension. This verse encourages humility, reminding us that our digital endeavors are part of a grander tapestry woven by the Maker of all things. Embracing the unknown is the essence of futuristic sowing.

11:6 -" Plant your seed in the morning and keep busy all afternoon, for you don't know if profit will come from one activity or another—or maybe both."

In this verse, Ecclesiastes urges us to maintain a constant rhythm of sowing and diligence. Our digital seeds, planted both morning and evening, reflect the ongoing nature of investment. The future's harvest may bring unexpected successes, and by keeping our hands active, we remain attuned to opportunities.

As we journey through Ecclesiastes 11, let's be mindful of these verses. Whether casting digital bread upon the waters, navigating winds of change, embracing the mysteries of creation, or maintaining rhythmic diligence, may our futuristic sowing yield a harvest beyond our wildest imaginations.

Applying its Wisdom

Ecclesiastes 11 serves as a guidebook for decision-making and futuristic investments. Let's embark on a journey through the verses of Ecclesiastes 11, applying its timeless wisdom to the art of crafting decisions that resonate with our future selves.

In the digital realm of decision-making, casting our efforts generously is like launching ventures into the waters. Consider decisions not only for immediate gains but with a foresight that envisions a bountiful harvest in the days to come. Our present choices, like digital bread, may return multiplied in the future.

Ecclesiastes 11 encourages diversification, mirroring the wisdom of spreading investments across various opportunities. By allocating resources to multiple endeavors, we prepare ourselves for unforeseen shifts, safeguarding our future selves from potential disasters.

In the landscape of decision-making, being overly cautious can hinder progress. Verse four urges us to avoid constant scrutiny and embrace a proactive approach. Just as a farmer must sow despite uncertainties, decisions for our future selves should not be paralyzed by the winds of doubt.

The rhythm of sowing morning and evening parallels the dynamic nature of decision-making. Continual diligence and activity ensure adaptability in the face of change. Embrace the uncertainty of the outcome, recognizing that both present and future choices contribute to harmonious success.

As we navigate the futuristic advice of Ecclesiastes 11, let's apply its wisdom to decision-making for our future selves. Whether casting digital bread, diversifying our efforts, avoiding excessive scrutiny, or maintaining rhythmic diligence, may our choices be guided by the understanding that decisions today echo through the corridors of time, shaping the destiny of our future selves.

Balancing Risk and Reward

Let's dive into the adventure of balancing risk and reward in both our personal and professional pursuits. Picture it like embarking on an epic journey through uncharted territories, where every decision shapes the landscape of your life. Balancing the thrill of risk with the sweet taste of reward is the secret sauce for a fulfilling odyssey.

1. **Personal Adventures:** When it comes to personal escapades, think of risk and reward as the dynamic duo guiding your path. Relationships, daring escapades, and self-discovery become your quests. Taking risks might mean stepping into the unknown, but the rewards? They unfold as personal growth, unforgettable experiences, and deep connections. Finding that sweet spot ensures your heart dances to the beat of your dreams.

2. **Professional Ventures:** In the professional arena, risk and reward become the architects of your career and ventures. Calculated risks—like exploring innovative projects, embracing challenges, or making strategic career moves—can lead to career growth, skill honing, and financial prosperity. Keeping these forces in check ensures your professional journey is an exciting expedition, not a blind leap into uncertainty.

3. **Navigating Life's Waves:** Envision life as a vast ocean with waves of opportunities and challenges. Balancing risk and reward is like skillfully navigating these waves. Too much caution might leave you stranded, missing out on the winds of change. Yet, diving headfirst into every risk might lead to choppy waters. Becoming a savvy sailor means harnessing the winds and steering through life's undulating tides.

4. **Constellations of Growth:** Each risk you take, whether personal or professional, contributes to the constellations on your life's canvas. These constellations tell stories of courage, resilience, and triumph. Rewards may not always be immediate, but over time, they weave into patterns of personal and professional growth that shimmer across your journey.

5. Equilibrium in Action: Striving for equilibrium involves weighing the gravitational forces of risk and reward in every decision. It's about making choices that align with your aspirations, and recognizing that venturing into the unknown is part of the thrilling dance of life. In this delicate balance lies the magic of a life well-lived—a life adorned with radiant constellations of fulfillment and success.

As you navigate the adventure of balancing risk and reward, embrace the uncertainty of your journey. Whether in your personal escapades or professional ventures, let your decisions be guided by the wisdom to find that perfect balance, ensuring your path is adorned with the brilliance of fulfilled dreams and achievements.

Discussion Questions with Self-Reflection
Here are some discussion questions along with self-reflection prompts to ponder the landscape of your future:

Casting Seeds:

How do you interpret the idea of "casting your bread upon the waters" in your personal and professional life?

Can you share an experience where taking a calculated risk led to unexpected but positive outcomes?

Diversifying Ventures:
In your current pursuits, do you tend to diversify your efforts or focus on one main endeavor? What are the advantages and disadvantages of your approach?

How might you apply the principle of diversification in your plans?

Navigating Uncertainty:
How comfortable are you with navigating uncertainties in your life? Share a specific situation where you embraced uncertainty and what you learned from it.

Do you find yourself waiting for the perfect conditions before making a decision? How has this impacted your journey?

Sowing and Reaping:
Reflect on a situation where you sowed seeds diligently, and the rewards took longer to materialize. How did you stay motivated during that time?

How can the concept of sowing and reaping apply to your current or future endeavors?

Balancing Present and Future:

How do you strike a balance between investing in your present and planning for your future? What adjustments, if any, could you make?

What specific actions can you take now that would positively impact your future self in 10 or 20 years?

Self-Reflection Prompts:

Personal Growth:

How do you envision your personal growth over the next decade? What aspects of your personality or skills would you like to develop?

Professional Aspirations :

Where do you see yourself professionally in 10 or 20 years? Are there specific industries or roles you aspire to explore?

Risk-Taking Tendencies:

Reflect on your comfort level with taking risks. Are there areas in your life where you might benefit from taking more calculated risks?

Learning from Mistakes:

Think about a past mistake or failure. What did you learn from that experience, and how has it influenced your decision-making?

Future Legacy:

Consider the legacy you want to leave behind. How can your current actions contribute to a positive legacy in the years to come?

Remember, these questions and reflections are your compass. Use them to navigate the journey of your life, making intentional choices that align with the stardust dreams of your future self.

Conclusion

As we bid adieu to the voyage through Chapter 11, our time machine prepares for one last trip, whisking us back to the present moment. The echoes of seeds cast upon waters, the dance with uncertainty, and the rhythms of sowing and reaping linger in the air, reminding us that our choices shape the very fabric of our existence.

Chapter 11 has been a guide, urging us to be intrepid Sowers, daring navigators of life's unpredictable seas. It's a call to embrace the unknown, diversify our ventures, and, above all, tend to the garden of our future selves with diligence and foresight.

As we return to the familiar terrain of the present, let's carry with us the wisdom gleaned from our odyssey. The lessons of risk and reward, the art of sowing in the morning and in the evening, all converge into a moment that tells the story of our journey.

And now, with a sense of purpose pulsating in our veins, we open the pages of Chapter 12 – the grand finale, the culmination of insights. This chapter beckons us to explore the very essence of living a life of purpose, inviting us to distill the symphony of wisdom into a melody that resonates with the core of our being.

So, fellow time-travelers, as we embark on this final leg of our expedition, let's savor the lessons of Chapter 11. Our journey has been a dance, a rhythmic exploration. And now, with purpose as our guiding star, we step into the pages of Chapter 12, ready to discover the quintessence of a life well-lived.

May this concluding chapter be the crescendo, the magnum opus, and the guiding light that leads us to live with intention, walk with purpose, and dance through time with grace. The time machine awaits, and the scrolls are unfurling once more. Onward to Chapter 12, where the essence of purpose awaits our eager exploration!

Chapter 12: Ecclesiastes 12 - Living a Life of Purpose: Applying Ecclesiastes in the 21st Century

Chapter 12 marks the grand finale of our journey, and it's all about living in the present moment. Imagine it as the spotlight on mindfulness, guiding us through the unpredictable scenes of life with an invitation to savor the richness of each instant.

Consider this chapter your ultimate mindfulness toolkit, equipping you to navigate the twists and turns of existence with grace. Living a purposeful life is like having a daily dose of mindful magic, transforming ordinary moments into extraordinary experiences.

So, fasten your seatbelts, time-travel enthusiasts! Chapter 12 isn't just a conclusion; it's an open door to unravel the secrets of mindful living. It's time to peel back the layers and discover the treasures hidden within the folds of our journey.

Get ready to immerse yourself in the present moment, fellow adventurers! Chapter 12 is not about chasing the future or dwelling in the past; it's about embracing the now with a grin on our faces and the anticipation of uncovering the mindful magic that makes life an awe-inspiring adventure!

Summarizing Key Lessons from Ecclesiastes 12

Ecclesiastes 12, the concluding chapter of this exploration, imparts profound lessons that resonate with contemporary living. Let's delve into key verses and draw reflections for our modern era:

12:1-3 - "Don't let the excitement of youth cause you to forget your Creator. Honor him in your youth before you grow old and say, "Life is not pleasant anymore." Remember him before the light of the sun, moon, and stars is dim to your old eyes, and rain clouds continually darken your sky. Remember him before your legs—the guards of your house—start to tremble; and before your shoulders—the strong men—stoop. Remember him before your teeth—your few remaining servants—stop grinding; and before your eyes—the women looking through the windows—see dimly."

Embrace mindfulness, acknowledging the significance of spirituality and purpose early in life, fostering a grounded foundation for the future.

12:6-7 - "Yes, remember your Creator now while you are young, before the silver cord of life snaps and the golden bowl is broken. Don't wait until the water jar is smashed at the spring and the pulley is broken at the well. For then the dust will return to the earth, and the spirit will return to God who gave it."

Recognize the brevity of life, inspiring a sense of urgency to live authentically, pursuing meaningful experiences over fleeting pleasures.

12:9-11 - "Keep this in mind: The Teacher was considered wise, and he taught the people everything he knew. He listened carefully to many proverbs, studying and classifying them. The Teacher sought to find just the right words to express truths clearly. The words of the wise are like cattle prods—painful but helpful. Their

collected sayings are like a nail-studded stick with which a shepherd drives the sheep."

Not only was the Teacher wise, but he also imparted knowledge to the people. Prioritize enduring wisdom over transient knowledge, recognizing the value of both acquiring and sharing insights for personal and societal growth.

12:12 - "But, my child, let me give you some further advice: Be careful, for writing books is endless, and much study wears you out. "Of making many books there is no end, and much study wearies the body."

Acknowledge the information overload in the modern age, emphasizing the need for discernment and focusing on meaningful knowledge that contributes to personal and collective well-being.

12:13-14 - "That's the whole story. Here now is my final conclusion: Fear God and obey his commands, for this is everyone's duty. ¹⁴ God will judge us for everything we do, including every secret thing, whether good or bad."

Fear God and keep his commandments, for this is the duty of all mankind. Uphold ethical principles, fostering a sense of accountability for one's actions and promoting a moral compass in personal and societal spheres.

Ecclesiastes 12 offers a roadmap for contemporary living, advocating for a balance between mindfulness, wisdom, ethical conduct, and a purposeful approach to life. Its verses resonate across time, providing a compass for navigating the complexities of our ever-evolving world.

Providing Practical Guidance

Applying the wisdom from Ecclesiastes to lead a meaningful and purposeful life in the 21st century involves integrating timeless principles with the complexities of our modern era. Here's some practical guidance:

Mindful Living:
Practice Mindfulness: Incorporate mindfulness into daily routines. Whether through meditation, breathing exercises, or simply being present, cultivate awareness of each moment.

Limit Distractions: Embrace technology intentionally. Set boundaries on screen time, notifications, and social media to foster genuine connections and reduce digital noise.

Wisdom in Decision-Making:
Seek Balanced Knowledge: Pursue knowledge that combines both traditional wisdom and contemporary insights. Evaluate information critically and discern between enduring truths and fleeting trends.

Mentorship: Engage in mentorship relationships, drawing on the wisdom of those with more experience. Similarly, mentor others, passing on valuable lessons.

Ethical Conduct:
Prioritize Integrity: Uphold ethical standards in personal and professional interactions. Prioritize honesty, fairness, and empathy in decision-making.

Social Responsibility: Engage in initiatives that contribute positively to society. Whether through volunteering, sustainable living, or ethical consumer choices, consider the broader impact of your actions.

Spirituality and Purpose:
Reflect on Life's Purpose: Regularly reflect on your life's purpose. What brings you joy, fulfillment, and a sense of meaning? Align your actions with these insights.

Spiritual Practices: Explore spiritual practices that resonate with you. This could include prayer, meditation, or other forms of connection with a higher purpose.

Balanced Work and Rest:
Set Boundaries: Establish clear boundaries between work and personal life. Prioritize self-care, ensuring adequate time for rest, recreation, and quality relationships.

Embrace Sabbatical Practices: Consider periodic breaks or sabbaticals to rejuvenate and gain fresh perspectives.
Continuous Personal Growth:

Lifelong Learning: Cultivate a mindset of continuous learning. Stay curious, explore new interests, and invest in personal development.

Adaptability: Embrace change and cultivate adaptability. Recognize that life is dynamic, and the ability to adapt ensures resilience in the face of challenges.

Community and Relationships:
Authentic Connections: Foster genuine connections with others. Prioritize quality over quantity in relationships, valuing authenticity and shared values.

Community Engagement: Participate in community initiatives, fostering a sense of belonging and contributing to the well-being of those around you.

Gratitude Practices:
Daily Gratitude: Incorporate daily gratitude practices. Reflecting on and expressing gratitude for small and significant aspects of life can enhance overall well-being.
Remember, the wisdom of Ecclesiastes invites a balanced and intentional approach to life. By integrating these practical steps, you can navigate the complexities of the 21st century while leading a purposeful and meaningful existence.

Encouragement to You
As we stand at the crossroads of our odyssey, let's take a moment to reflect on the winding paths we've traversed, the peaks we've scaled, and the valleys we've navigated. Your journey, with all its twists and turns, is uniquely yours—a tapestry woven with the threads of triumphs, challenges, and moments that define who you are.

In the quiet moments of reflection, ask yourself: What brings a spark to your soul? What moments have left an indelible mark on your heart? In the grand narrative of your life, where do you find purpose, meaning, and resonance?

Consider the footprints you've left on the sands of time. What stories do they tell, and what lessons have you gathered along the way? Each step, each detour, contributes to the mosaic of your existence.

Purpose, elusive yet ever-present, resides in the authenticity of your connections, the impact of your actions, and the alignment of your journey with the core of your being. Reflect on the whispers of your heart, for within them lies the guidance to your true purpose.

In this reflection, embrace the evolution you've undergone. Growth often emerges from the fertile soil of challenges, and resilience is the echo of your spirit bouncing back from setbacks. Celebrate the victories, no matter how small, and honor the lessons gleaned from trials.

As you ponder your journey and purpose, remember that the quest for meaning is an ongoing exploration—a journey, not a destination. Your purpose may evolve, shape-shift, and reveal itself in unexpected ways. Stay attuned to the symphony of your desires, passions, and dreams.

So, dear reader, take a moment to appreciate the uniqueness of your expedition. In the mirror of introspection, recognize the strength you've discovered, the wisdom you've gained, and the beauty that emanates from your narrative.

May your reflections be a compass guiding you toward a future where each step is intentional, each decision resonates with authenticity, and each moment is embraced with purpose.

With curiosity as your guide and purpose as your North Star, continue to dance through the intricate choreography of your journey. The adventure unfolds not just in the destination but in the steps, you take and the meaning you infuse into each stride.

Onward, intrepid traveler, to a future illuminated by the purpose you cultivate and the reflections that shape your ongoing narrative.

Discussion Questions & Reflective Moments

Reflecting on Your Journey:

What pivotal moments in your life journey stand out the most to you, and why?

How have your experiences, both positive and challenging, shaped the person you are today?

Defining Purpose:

In your own words, what does the concept of "purpose" mean to you?

Have there been moments in your life where you felt a strong sense of purpose? What were those moments?

Learning from Challenges:

Can you recall a challenging experience that, in hindsight, taught you valuable lessons or contributed to personal growth?

How do you approach setbacks, and what resilience strategies do you employ to bounce back from challenges?

Values and Authenticity:
Identify three values that are central to who you are. How do these values align with the choices you make in your life?

In what ways do you express your authenticity in your daily actions and interactions?

Aligning Actions with Purpose:
Consider your daily activities and commitments. How well do they align with your sense of purpose?

Are there adjustments or changes you could make to better align your actions with your perceived purpose?

Celebrating Victories:
Reflect on personal achievements, no matter how small. How do these victories contribute to your sense of fulfillment?
How do you celebrate your successes, and do you take time to acknowledge your accomplishments?

Evolution and Growth:
Think about how you've evolved over the years. What aspects of your character or beliefs have undergone significant changes?

How do you view personal growth, and what role does continuous learning play in your life?

Future Aspirations:
Envision your future self. What qualities, accomplishments, or experiences do you aspire to have in the next phase of your journey?

How can your reflections on your past and present guide the intentional steps you take toward your envisioned future?

These questions are designed to prompt deep reflection on your journey and purpose. Take the time to ponder each question, jot down your thoughts, and use these reflective moments to gain insights into your narrative.

Conclusion

As we draw the curtain on this captivating journey through the corridors of Ecclesiastes and the musings on life, purpose, and meaning, let's take a collective breath and savor the richness of our exploration.

Our quest has been a tapestry woven with the threads of ancient wisdom, timeless insights, and the vibrant hues of your unique reflections. From the cyclical rhythms of life to the pursuit of wisdom, from the challenges of the modern age to the embrace of uncertainties, each chapter has unfolded a new layer of understanding.

In this final chapter, we stood at the crossroads of our narratives, inviting introspection and contemplation about the essence of our journey and the purpose that resides within us. You, dear reader, have been an integral part of this odyssey, and your reflections have added depth and diversity to the collective tapestry we've created.

As we bid farewell to Ecclesiastes, let's not view it as an end but as a launching pad—a launch into a life infused with purpose, mindfulness, and a commitment to continuous growth. The wisdom imparted isn't confined to the pages of a book but serves as a compass for the ongoing adventure of self-discovery.

In the grand finale of our conversation, consider these parting thoughts: Your journey is a masterpiece in progress, and each step forward is a brushstroke adding to the canvas of your existence. The pursuit of meaning isn't a one-time event but a perpetual dance—a rhythmic ballet of introspection, learning, and purposeful living.

As you close this chapter, remember that your story continues. You are the author, the protagonist, and the narrator of your epic. May the wisdom gleaned from Ecclesiastes be a guiding star in the vast cosmos of your future endeavors.

This isn't a farewell; it's an invitation. An invitation to carry the torch of wisdom, to keep seeking, questioning, and living with intention. Our journey through Ecclesiastes is but one chapter in the library of life, and there are countless more volumes awaiting exploration.

So, dear reader, go forth with the echoes of Ecclesiastes resonating in your heart. May your journey be filled with purpose, your reflections be profound, and your story be an inspiration to others.

Until we meet again in the pages of another adventure!

Beyond Ecclesiastes - Further Study and Reflection

Where We Have Been

As we fasten our seatbelts and embark on this journey through Ecclesiastes, let's take a moment to hit rewind and recap the highlights. Picture it like a time-traveling adventure, hopping in our trusty time machine once again and zipping through the chapters of ancient wisdom.

Chapter 1: Ecclesiastes kicked off like the opening scene of a time-travel movie. Life's a loop, like the endless sunrise and sunset. It's like the universe's original algorithm, reminding us that our latest viral post is just a tiny blip in the feed.

Chapter 2: We punched in the coordinates for modern-day work life. Ecclesiastes dropped some truth bombs about career goals. Climbing the corporate ladder might be like running on a treadmill without an off switch. Who knew success could be such a puzzle?

Chapter 3: Next stop – the beat of time. Ecclesiastes 3 was like a dance party of life's events. Joy and sorrow, likes and dislikes, all mixed into a grand choreography. It was the ultimate mixtape of existence.

Chapter 4: Time for a selfie in Ecclesiastes 4. It's all about ditching the vanity of comparisons in the age of filters and Facetime. Remember, the real masterpiece is in genuine connections, not pixel-perfect snapshots.

Chapter 5: Ecclesiastes 5 – the planetary pledge. In a world dominated by climate change talks, this chapter whispered about our vows to protect our homes. It's a reminder that even small eco-friendly choices can send ripples through the universe.

Chapter 6: Ecclesiastes 6 – the galactic pursuit of wealth. Brace yourself for a reality check. Chasing material gains without true fulfillment? Ecclesiastes reflects on the hollowness of that wild bling chase.

Chapter 7: Welcome to the poker game in Ecclesiastes 7. Cards are dealt with an unpredictable hand, urging us to embrace the unexpected. It's like a wild card in the deck, making life's surprises more exhilarating.

Chapter 8: Ecclesiastes 8 – the quasar of wisdom. Dive into the stratosphere of intellect. In a world drowning in information, Ecclesiastes suggests sifting through the noise for timeless insights.

Chapter 9: Cosmic equalizer alert! Ecclesiastes 9 unfolds the universal truth that time and chance don't play favorites. It's like a reminder that everyone gets a shot on the stage, no matter our roles in the lifelong drama.

Chapter 10: Ecclesiastes 10 navigates us through the minefield of decision-making. It's like a manual for avoiding blunders and making enlightened choices in the information overload era.

Chapter 11: Picture Ecclesiastes 11 as the stock market of life. Every decision and every investment shapes our portfolio. It's a call to weigh risks and rewards, making choices that echo through the balance sheet of our existence.

Chapter 12: Ecclesiastes 12 isn't just a finale; it's the climax, the zenith, the magnum opus of wisdom. It's like the ultimate guide to living a life of purpose, a roadmap to grace and intention.

As we close the time-travelling scroll of Ecclesiastes, it's not the end; it's a launchpad for further exploration. Think of it like the end of a blockbuster movie – a teaser for sequels and spin-offs awaiting your exploration.

So, fellow time travelers, as you flip through the pages of Ecclesiastes, may its wisdom be your North Star in the timeless quest for understanding. Until our time-travelling paths cross again, keep pondering, keep seeking, and keep dancing through the cosmic rhythms of time and space.

Further Study

Congratulations on completing your journey through Ecclesiastes! If you're eager to dive deeper into the wisdom of this timeless text and explore related themes, here's a curated list of books, podcasts, and videos that can further enrich your understanding:

Books:

"The Message of Ecclesiastes" by Derek Kidner:

A concise and insightful commentary that provides a detailed analysis of Ecclesiastes, offering valuable perspectives on its meaning.

"Ecclesiastes: Why Everything Matters" by Philip G. Ryken:

This book delves into the relevance of Ecclesiastes in the modern world, exploring its themes of purpose, meaning, and the pursuit of wisdom.

"The Book of Ecclesiastes" by Tremper Longman III:

Longman's in-depth exploration of Ecclesiastes offers a scholarly yet accessible examination of its literary, historical, and theological aspects.

"Living Life Backward: How Ecclesiastes Teaches Us To Live In Light Of The End" by David Gibson

This book explores the book of Ecclesiastes and sheds light on how to live knowing that one thing is for certain.

Podcasts:

"The Bible Project Podcast" - Episode on Ecclesiastes:

The Bible Project offers an engaging and visually rich exploration of biblical themes. Their podcast episode on Ecclesiastes provides valuable insights.

"Exploring My Strange Bible" - Ecclesiastes Series by Tim Mackie:

Tim Mackie, one of the creators of The Bible Project, provides a deep dive into Ecclesiastes in this podcast series, offering both theological and practical perspectives.

Videos:

"Ecclesiastes: Wisdom for Living Well" by The Bible Project:

The Bible Project's animated videos are visually captivating and intellectually stimulating. Their video on Ecclesiastes provides a great overview of the book.

"Ecclesiastes Explained" by John Piper:

John Piper, a respected theologian, shares his insights into the themes and teachings of Ecclesiastes in this video, offering a thoughtful perspective.

Further Study:

Join Online Bible Study Groups:

Platforms like Bible Study Fellowship (BSF) or small groups on platforms like Meetup or Facebook can offer communal exploration of Ecclesiastes.

Explore Online Theological Courses:

Platforms like Coursera, Udemy, or The Great Courses often have courses on biblical studies that could include in-depth modules on Ecclesiastes.

Remember, the journey of exploration is as personal as it is communal. Feel free to mix and match resources based on your preferences and learning style. May these suggestions inspire further curiosity and understanding on your ongoing adventure of biblical exploration!

Continue Exploring

Congratulations on reaching the end of our adventure through Ecclesiastes! But guess what? Our journey doesn't have to stop here. There's a whole world of wisdom waiting for us to discover, and I invite you to keep exploring.

Why not take a moment each day to ponder the timeless truths we've uncovered? Consider how they might shape your decisions, guide your relationships, and bring purpose to your life. Think of it like finding treasures that make your journey through each day a bit brighter.

And you know what's even better? As we grow individually, we also contribute to the well-being of our communities. Share these nuggets of wisdom with friends, family, or anyone who might need a bit of encouragement. Imagine the positive ripples we can create together!

So, grab a cup of your favorite drink, find a cozy spot, and let the adventure continue. Whether it's a quiet reflection, a chat with a friend, or exploring more books and resources, let's keep the journey going.

Here's to your personal growth and our collective well-being!

God Bless!

About the Author

Debb Boom Wateren [aka D B Wateren] loves helping other people learn. She has done this in her time as an ESL educator, guiding many others through the joys and travails of learning English, and in her time as a project manager, navigating construction projects from concept to completion. A lifelong learner, she enjoys art, music, travel, history, reading, and libraries. She has a symbiotic learning relationship with her cat, Eleanor Roosevelt, named for one of her heroes. They both enjoy their home in the High Rocky Mountains, embracing life's new challenges together. Says Debb, "Attitude is the difference between an ordeal and an adventure." The originator of that quote is unknown, but Debb embraces it all the same.

DBW Best Books LLC
contact@dbwbestbooks.com

Thank you for reading and learning from this book. Please consider leaving an honest review.

Other Books by D B Wateren

Non-Fiction
Women Adventures and Explorers
Women Inventors, Scientists, and Discoverers
Women Breaking Barriers in Sport
Women Leaders in History
Proverbs for the 21st Century
Psalms for the 21st Century
Ecclesiastes for the 21st Century
Reimagining Matthew for the 21st Century
Marked for Today: A Contemporary Exploration of the Gospel o Mark for the 21st Century
Lucid Horizons: Navigating the Gospel of Luke in the 21st Century
The Game of Cricket for Spectators

Journals
Kindness: A Choice We Make Each Day
Travel Journal
Wine Tasting Journal
Prayer Journal
Writing Journals with Blank Pages
Daily Planner for Teens
Daily Planner for Adults: Flower Drawings to Inspire

Coloring Books and Activity Books for Adults
Fancy Decorated Eggs
Fantasy Animals and Birds
Elaborate Animals
Mandalas Book 1 and 2
Mazes
Picture Searches Book 1 and 2
Gnomes and Elves
Flower Gardens

Coloring Books for Children
Large Wild Birds
Construction
Firefighters
Music
Fun Animals
Space: Ages 4-8
Space: Ages 8-11
Gnomes and Elves and Where They Live

Made in the USA
Columbia, SC
18 October 2024

6ff611b4-8edb-40e9-8d6a-37865b4e8700R01